Rise Up, Wise Up

Thanks to Jane for her love
and no-nonsense advice

To Tim Snowdon
for the photo on the back

And to all the following
for inspirational ideas
and week-by-week work

Louisa Akin-Smith
Jane Blazeby
Sue Doggett
Mark Fenton
Jo Frost
Sally Hanks
Dan Johnson
Martina Jones
John Lawrie
Al Massey
Ali Mawhinney
John Owen
Hazel Sumner
Billie Thaw
Dan Thaw
Berj Topalian
Duncan Watts
Wendy Watts
Kate Welham

The voice of the Lord strikes with flashes of lightning

Psalm 29:7 (NIV)

RISE UP, WISE UP

NICK JONES

Published by
The Bible Reading Fellowship
Peter's Way, Sandy Lane West
Oxford, England
ISBN 0 7459 3259 2
Albatross Books Pty Ltd
PO Box 320, Sutherland
NSW 2232, Australia
ISBN 0 7324 0957 8

First edition 1996
10 9 8 7 6 5 4 3 2 1 0

Acknowledgments
Unless otherwise stated, scripture is quoted from
the **Good News Bible**, published by The Bible
Societies/HarperCollins Publishers Ltd., UK, ©
American Bible Society, 1966, 1971, 1976, 1992

The Holy Bible, New International Version (NIV), ©
1973, 1978, 1984 by International Bible Society. Used
by permission.

The poem 'Best Friends' on page 72 is copyright © Adrian Henri.
Reproduced by permission of the author c/o Rogers, Coleridge & White Ltd.,
20 Powis Mews, London,W11 1JN. From *The Phantom Lollipop Lady*,
Methuen, 1986.

Cover photograph: Zefa UK

A catalogue record for this book is available
from the British Library

Printed and bound in Malta

Contents

Here are proverbs that will help you to recognize wisdom and good advice, and understand sayings with deep meaning. They can teach you how to live intelligently and how to be honest, just, and fair. They can make an inexperienced person clever and teach young people how to be resourceful.

Proverbs 1:2–4

etter to Leaders

Do you ever wish that God would work in your life in an even just slightly dramatic way? So there would be no question about it? I sometimes do. When I hear about the wonderful things that God has done in the lives of other Christians I naturally wonder why I don't seem to have the same experiences. Perhaps I don't have enough faith. With not a little embarrassment I remember one occasion a few years ago when I earnestly tried to have more faith. It had become apparent that the engine of our car was in serious and expensive trouble. Clouds of smoke poured out the exhaust pipe. So I parked in a lay-by, switched off the engine, prayed that God would fix it, and tried to have faith that he would. He didn't. Well, at least not directly; the garage did it and charged the going rate.

In the Bible we get a selective account of the highlights of God's relationship with human beings. (The most significant of these moments are explored in the 'Out of This World' teaching material.) Naturally we tend to focus on and remember the more spectacular examples of God's interventions in human history; the times when God ZAPPED human beings. These kind of events, however, form the minority of the human race's everyday experience of God. Though God does ZAP us, he also expects us to get on with living for him to the best of our ability in the daily routine of life. He has equipped us for this very well by giving us common sense and the ability to think for ourselves.

In Proverbs we have a record of human beings looking at the world, reflecting on what they see, and using their common sense to learn how to live wisely. It is a collection of sound, sensible, and down to earth sayings that have a lot to teach us. Though God ***is*** a God who ZAPS, he tends not to ZAP us when we are quite capable of taking appropriate action ourselves, (like taking the car to the garage). He wants us to rise up, wise up and make the most of the gifts and abilities he has given us. That is the message of Proverbs and if we take it on board ourselves and pass it on to our young people we will have given them a solid foundation in life.

Introducing Proverbs

The book of Proverbs is a record of the wisdom and experience of many generations condensed into sparklingly fresh short sayings. King Solomon wrote the majority of these Proverbs, the remainder being gathered from a wide range of sources and authors by the book's editor with the specific objective of providing a thorough educational programme for young and less experienced people. He introduces his wisdom manual like this: *'Here are proverbs that will help you to recognise wisdom and good advice, and understand sayings with de meaning. They can teach you how to live intelligently and how to be honest, just, and fair. They c make an inexperienced person clever and teach young people how to be resourceful.'* Proverbs 1:2–4

What marks Proverbs (and the Bible's other 'Wisdom' literature) out from the rest of the Ol Testament is the fact that the sage looks at life from a very different perspective from the prie or prophet. He isn't concerned with the great Old Testament themes of redemption and covenant. Instead he deals with the wisdom or folly of individuals' attitudes and actions in the ordinary things of life. Proverbs is packed with prudent advice about parents, honesty, the wa we speak and think, friendship, and business. As we explore each of these areas we are agair and again forced to consider the question, 'Am I being wise or foolish? Am I being wise or foolish in my business dealings, in my relationship with my parents, with my words?' The edit of the book of Proverbs is determined to help his readers to live wisely in every area of life.

Though the advice of Proverbs is utterly down to earth it in no way excludes God. The sage believes that common sense is the greater part of wisdom, but he is also entirely convinced t a wise and good life is lived in accordance with God's principles. He states right at the beginn that the key to a well-lived life is to have reverence for the Lord and to trust him fully. That belief is the foundation of the book.

Human beings don't really change and the wisdom of three thousand years ago is still relevan today. What was a manual for the young and less experienced of yester-millennium is still a working manual for us now. May it teach us all *'to live intelligently and how to be honest, just a fair.'*

triking Out

The following hints will explain to you
What youthwork's about and what leaders should do.

I decided to follow Jesus as a teenager, as did my wife Jane. According to a recent report commissioned by the General Synod of the Church of England, sixty-five per cent of adult Christians took 'significant steps towards faith before the age of thirteen'.[1] We, like the majority of Christians, are living proof that youthwork can have a lifelong impact, and are both immensely grateful to those people who patiently sowed and watered the seeds of faith in our lives. With the enormous range of influences on young people today it is particularly important that we provide good youth groups where young people can investigate and meet God for themselves.

It was as very inexperienced youth leaders, aged twenty-five and twenty-three, that Jane and I agreed to take on the running of our church's group for eleven to fourteen-year-olds. Not surprisingly we made, and have continued to make, many mistakes in the six years since. The following hints on leading a youth group are a distillation of the lessons we have learnt. We hope that they will save you and your group some of the pain that comes from learning by trial and error and will equip you to do the job well.

Using me?

Whether you are considering youth work from a distance or are in it up to your neck, I would like you to spend a little time thinking about the following two questions.

- Is your relationship with God alive and growing?
- Do you like young people and want to help them to meet God?

I believe that these are vital qualities in a youthworker and that your answer should really be 'yes' to each question. A love for God is 'caught not taught' so it is important that you as a leader are in love with God and dependent on his Holy Spirit. Don't be daunted by this, but try to walk closely with God and in your busyness make sure you don't neglect your own need for fellowship and teaching.

Hint one: love

The most important thing that you can do for any young person is to show them God's love by caring about them. This is the most powerful visual aid in youthwork. You don't need to be young and attractive with your finger on the pulse of contemporary youth culture to be a good youth leader. What your group members want to know is whether you care about them, whether you like them and are interested in them. One of the most effective leaders we have ever had in our team was a wonderful silver-haired and godly lady in her fifties. The young people in our group loved her because they instinctively knew that she cared about them and was interested in the things that made up their lives; they could talk to her about anything.

Of course good teaching is important, but in the balance of influences it is easily outweighed by the influence of practical love. To demonstrate this, try listing six sermons, talks or meetings that have played a significant part in your growth as a Christian. Then list six people who have played a key role in your Christian life. I am sure that the second list will more easily come to mind. The most effective way in which we communicate the truths and reality of the Christian faith is not the way we teach them, but the way we live. If our young people feel that we respect, accept and care about them and if they can see that our relationship with God is real they will begin to believe that God is real too. So get t know your group members and let them get to know you. Arrange outings, take them the swimming pool or invite them round to your home for a pizza and video.

As the group gets to know you, they will observe all that goes on, and particularly the way in which the leaders relate to each other. Christian love and friendship should be seen in the leadership team. The other day we asked our young people to complete a questionnaire about the group. One of the questions asked what they would remembe about the group in seventy years' time. We were touched by the response of one pers who replied, 'the laughing leaders'.

Hint two: prayer

Prayer is a vital part of youthwork. Surround all your work and planning with prayer. Pr for the young people in your group. Pray for any other leaders in your team. Pray with the other leaders in your team. Put them all on a prayer rota so that you pray for them weekly. Beyond that seek out a number of people in the church who will commit them selves to praying for your group and its leaders. Keep them regularly informed about what to pray for either in a prayer letter or over the phone. Get your prayer requests printed in the church prayer diary or on its service sheet.

Hint three: teaching

Jesus was an outstanding teacher—enthusiastic, clear and inspiring. I often wonder how we can become like that. Think back to your school days. What made the good teache stand out from the rest? I was inspired by the teachers who knew and loved their subje and had a real desire to help their students understand and enjoy it. Invariably they mad every effort to bring their subject to life and were prepared to spend extra time helping their students get to grips with it.

If your group sense that you love God, are excited by following Jesus and really want them to discover God's love for themselves, then you are already more than half-way there.

The next chapter deals with the practicalities of 'how' to teach well and all the 'Lightning Bolts' material has been designed to help you explore the Bible and the Christian faith with your group in a relevant, positive and exciting way.

Well, actually Vicar
it's not going too well!
ZZZ
ZZZ
ZZZ
ZZZ

Hint four: church backing

Youthwork is a key part of the work of the wider church. So make sure that the leaders of your church know what you are up to and are behind you in your aims and objectives. They should take an interest in what you are doing and support you. However, it may be more practical for them to nominate a senior member of the church to oversee what you are doing and to whom you are accountable. This person should be concerned for your spiritual growth and personal welfare just as you are concerned for the spiritual growth and personal needs of your leaders and young people. Meet with them regularly, pray together and keep them informed about how it's going. If your church is unable to arrange this for you ask a friend to support you or get your fellowship or house group to do it.

Hint five: building up a leadership team

Any group with more than ten members will probably need more than one leader. We find that the ideal leader—group-member ratio is roughly one to six, preferably matched sex to sex. We have found working with other leaders and managing our team one of the most rewarding and enjoyable parts of youthwork. As overall leader your main responsibility is to the other members of your team. Care for them, train them, teach them, set them a good example. Perhaps you could eat a meal together once a month when you plan and pray for the group. Keep in touch with how things are going with each of them at home, at work and with God. Be sensitive to the other pressures on your leaders; lighten their load when they have exams or increased pressure at work or home. Do let them know that you appreciate them; perhaps send them a postcard from your holidays or a small present at Christmas and don't forget to say 'thank you' regularly. A happy le ership team leads to a happy youth group.

We have given the whole process of enlisting new leaders a great deal of thought. This our method. Start by praying, and sending out some prayer requests to anyone who prays for your group. Ask your leaders to see if they have any friends who might be int ested or see if there is anyone you know. Potentially this is a very fruitful avenue to pur sue; most of our leaders past and present have come through this route. Ask the churc leaders if they know of anyone who might be suitable. Possibly give out a request for h in a church service explaining what is needed and what is involved. You may be surpris by some of the people that turn up, but if they have the following qualities they most d nitely have the potential to become a good youth leader:

- a living relationship with God
- an ability to get on with young people
- enthusiasm, willingness to learn and enough time

Arrange a time to chat with or 'interview' any potential candidates. You need to know about their experience, suitability, compatibility with the present team, their aims and ambitions, weaknesses and background. Consider asking for a reference. Remember th your responsibility is to the young people in your care. This 'interview' equally gives the potential leader the chance to find out about you and the job. Pray together and if appr priate offer them a trial period of say four weeks. This is a good opportunity for you bo to take a more in-depth look at each other and the group. Do make it clear that both sides can say 'no' at the end of the four weeks. We have had very few leaders with whom the feelings haven't been mutual.

Assuming that you both decide that they should join the team ask them to commit ther selves to the work for a minimum period of time, perhaps a year. Make it clear that the can always come and ask if they are not sure about anything or are having problems. Keep a friendly eye on them and perhaps regularly meet up and review how things are going. Don't drop them in the deep end, but let them gradually gain experience at lead groups and doing things 'up front'. Remember to give them plenty of encouragement a positive feedback.

Hint six: the right environment

Make every effort to think of ways of making your meeting room more friendly. Think about the seating arrangements—chairs, floor or mats? Think about the wall and ceiling space and whether you could use them for visual aids. Think about the temperature, lighting and privacy. Consider whether it is worth trying to change rooms. Providing a comfortable environment will make the world of difference. Perhaps you could get you group involved in transforming your room. Over the years we have accumulated all so of visual aids and junk which we have lying around most of the time. This makes the room a bit like a treasure trove and the young people absorb important information jus by being there.

If you live near the church and have a small group perhaps you could try meeting in yo home. The young people are guaranteed to enjoy it.

Hint seven: parents

Getting to know the parents of your group members will help you understand their fam background. It also enables the parents to get to know you and have the confidence to entrust their children into your care. They will only do this if they feel sure that you are responsible and competent. So be courteous and friendly and keep them informed abo what is going on with programme cards, notes on outing times and dates, and plenty of advance warning. Always be meticulous about all aspects of safety and hygiene. Communicating with parents who are not Christians is particularly important as they may be concerned about their child's involvement with the church.

Hint eight: a clear aim

The reason for having an aim for your group is to achieve it. Without an aim you risk achieving nothing. The aim of our group is that every member has a positive and enjoyable encounter with the Christian faith. Our leaders know this and whenever we lose our way we come back to it. So decide on a sentence that sums up the reason for your group's existence. It will be an invaluable help as you make decisions about all aspects of the group's life.

It is also helpful to set yourself short-term objectives. For example, if you are just starting out you might set yourself the objective of establishing a regular group within six months. The leaders of a growing group might set themselves the objective of building up a leadership team or getting their group members reading the Bible at home.

In conclusion

Young people matter to God. They are his children and he longs for them to come to know him, but he needs people like you to introduce him to them and help them to grow. If you are willing, God will use you in some very exciting ways, some of which you will never have even imagined. At times it will be tough, and you will frequently be disappointed, but don't give up. You are doing a vital job that is treasured by God.

Nick and Jane

Running a Meeting

Running a meeting, large, medium or small: The following tips apply to them all.

Your week-by-week meetings are a fantastic window of opportunity through which Go can touch the lives of your group members, so make the most of the time. The memb of your group will probably spend the 168 hours of their week something like this: 65 hours asleep, 40 hours at school, 35 hours at home, 12 hours of television, 10 hours w friends, 5 hours eating, but only 1 hour at your youth group. That hour or so may ever be the only contact some of the members of your group have with the Christian faith.

The following ten tips will help you to lead your meetings well and so maximize their impa They all apply whether you are leading a small discussion group or a larger group meeting.

Members of larger youth groups will benefit from the opportunity to spend part of eac week's meeting in smaller cells. Do arrange this if at all possible. This is often where the real work is done. In small groups your young people can explore and chat through the subject, pray together and get to know each other and their leader. The other advantag of regular small groups is that each leader is identified with a handful of young people fo whom they can pray and have a special concern.

The first five tips are concerned with preparation for the meeting, and the second five with personal 'on the day' leadership skills.

Tip one: plan ahead

Start planning the next meeting well before it happens. Meet with the other members c the team the week before and plan and pray together. Make sure that you are all clear about the aim of the meeting and discuss exactly what will be taught so that you are all saying the same thing. Arrange who will lead the main part, who is going to do what, ar whose responsibility it is to get props and equipment together.

Tip two: pray

Prayer is a vital part of your preparation. Spend time praying both on your own and with the other leaders. Pray for the meeting: that God would use all that you have planned. Pray for the other leaders and the parts they will be playing. Pray for the group members, preferably by name: that God would speak to them through what you do.

Tip three: know your subject

Make sure that you understand the essential facts about your subject, or the plot of the story that you are teaching, and know how to explain them simply. You don't have to have a thorough grasp of the varying branches of theological insight on the topic, but you do need to understand the basics and what they mean to you, whether it be the Holy Spirit, Balaam's ass, or prayer.

Tip four: be ready

On the day arrive early and allow plenty of time to get everything organized and ready well before your group arrives. Run through any sketches, talks and the general plan for the meeting before the group descend upon you. Make sure that you have all the equipment you need—Bibles, pens, paper—and that you know where you have put them. Spend the limited time you have with your group members concentrating on them and not trying to find the sonic infra-red X-ray specs that you need for the Bible reading.

Tip five: get the group involved

We all learn best by 'doing'. All of us remember far more of what we 'do' than what we just 'hear' or 'see'. So get the young people involved in the meeting wherever possible, with readings, sketches, music or artwork; anything that they would enjoy, even just helping to set up the room.

Tip six: create a relaxed atmosphere

Creating a relaxed atmosphere in your group takes time. The key is to be relaxed yourself: it's contagious. Start by standing near the door and individually welcoming the group members by name and with a big smile as they arrive. Have some other leaders milling around to chat to the group and particularly any new people. The first time I went to a youth group I left within three minutes because no one spoke to me. I tried again a few weeks later and to my astonishment was greeted by a friendly face who even knew my name; after that I never looked back. Make every effort to get to know each person's name and use it. This is a very practical way of showing that you care and, as I found out, makes the world of difference.

Seating arrangements are also an important part of creating a relaxed atmosphere. In a large meeting encourage everyone to sit close together, rather than spread out round the room. In small discussion groups get everyone sitting in a circle so they can all see each other. Don't let little clusters sit in opposite corners or behind each other. Use comfy chairs if possible, or sit on the floor, perhaps on mats.

An important way of creating a relaxed atmosphere in small groups is to let the group chat with each other. Start your small group times by asking how their week has been and what they have been up to. Remember that the young people will be more shy than you so it's up to you to take the initiative in conversation and in directing the meeting. Let the quiet and shy individuals stay quiet; if you don't put pressure on them they will, in time, come out of themselves and get more involved in the group.

Tip seven: learn to listen

An essential part of leading a small group is listening to the group members. This come naturally to some, but we can all learn to do it better. Learn to listen to snippets of cor versation and throw-away remarks and, when appropriate, pick up on these either at t time or later. They can tell you about what is going on in a young person's life and can sometimes be tentative requests for help. During activities listen thoughtfully to the gro members' comments about what you are doing and never interrupt them. Always foc your full attention on the person to whom you are talking.

Tip eight: be enthusiastic

Enthusiasm is infectious and will soon spread among the members of your group. Be enthusiastic about the activities you are doing and don't plan anything for the group tha you don't find interesting and can't be enthusiastic about.

Tip nine: a note on discipline

In theory, if you are well-prepared and give your group a stimulating and action-packec programme they won't have either the time or inclination to muck around. Trouble is likely to arise if the young people are bored or not interested. However, the group ca be hard to handle when, through no fault of your own, they are gripped by a collectiv 'bad mood' or reckless over-excitability. Personally I would rather have a noisy group v are obviously enjoying themselves and involved in what we are doing than a 'well-behaved' group who just sit there in silence. However, you may also have the odd ind vidual who seems determined to disrupt your meeting despite your best efforts. Don't them spoil the meeting for the rest of the group. Here are some suggestions to help y deal with any situations like this:

- Get another leader to sit by the child throughout the meeting. Their very presence should be a restraining influence, but they could also pray for the child and where necessary have a word in their ear.
- Have a quiet 'man to man' or 'woman to woman' type conversation with the young person afterwards. Find out how they feel about the meetings and try to get them on your side.
- Try to get them involved in the meeting. Perhaps they could take part in a sketch, or preparing some visual aids, anything that will help to make them feel valued and perhaps a little more responsible.

It is often true that a young person who is 'causing trouble' in the group is particularly in need of your love and encouragement. Try to see this as an opportunity, not a problem.

Susan, when you've finished tying up the boys could you tell us what we learnt last week...

Tip ten: take stock

Naturally, and for a variety of reasons, some meetings will go better than others so don't be discouraged if you seem to be taking a while to learn the art of leading a meeting (it took us years and we're still learning). At the end of each meeting try and work out whether you achieved your aim for the meeting. Ask yourself why it was that you did or didn't succeed. Try and put what you learn into practice next time. When things don't go quite as you hoped, talk to God about it and ask for his help. Chat with your other leaders and perhaps a member of the church leadership. Above all, keep going because, whether you realize it or not, God will still be at work drawing the young people to himself.

Nick and Jane

How to Use 'Lightning Bolts'

A quick tour round the layout of this book,
The what, why and how—and where you should look.

There are two elements to each title in 'Lightning Bolts': the leaders' guides and the da Bible reading notes. They both explore the same theme or book from the Bible and c be used together or apart. The leaders' guides provide you with ten complete meetin plans full of clear ideas of ways to communicate and unpack the message of the Bible v both small and large groups. Each meeting plan contains the following elements:

Leaders' information

The aim

A clearly expressed aim for the meeting.

The lightning bolt

The Bible passage on which the meeting is based.

Equipment checklist

A list of equipment needed for the meeting.

Letter to leaders

A personal introduction to the subject of the meeting along with one or two thought-provoking questions to help you apply it to your life.

Ideas for the meeting

Each of the different ideas or activities suggested for each meeting falls into one of the following eight categories and will always be identified by its symbol. The first four are 'presentations' to the group and are usually suggested for use when your group is all together. The second four are 'activities' for the group members and so are more suita for smaller discussion groups, though some of them could be used with larger groups. They are, however, all loosely interchangeable so that you can pick and mix in the light your group's needs and the amount of space and time that you have available.

Presentations

Sparking off

Presentations that introduce and set the scene for the meeting.

The main bolt

The Bible passage presented or experienced.

Shock waves

Presentations exploring the implications of 'The main bolt' and how it is relevant today.

In a flash

The main point of the meeting summed up in a flash.

Activities

Charging up

Ice-breaker activities to get the group members charged up and ready.

Explosions

Activities in which the group members explore and unpack the Bible passage together.

Striking home

Activities that help the group take the point of the meeting on board and, if appropriate, apply it to their lives.

Return strikes

An opportunity for the group to pray together.

Rise Up, Wise Up Special Features

The People on the Pavement

Street Wise?
2 mins

If you have ever seen TV programmes in which a roving reporter asks randomly selected members of the public for their views on a chosen topic then you will understand the idea behind the *People on the Pavement* feature. Each meeting starts with a clip of tape in which tw or three *People on the Pavement* answer a question on the subject of the meeting. Meeting o for example, explores the question, *'What is the most important thing you can do in life?'* and that is the question the *People on the Pavement* try to answer.

As well as setting the scene for the meeting the *People on the Pavement* feature also teaches t group members to ask that 'proverbial' recurring question 'Are you being wise or foolish?' Pa the tape after each *Person on the Pavement* has spoken and ask the group members to vote with a show of hands on whether they think the answer given was wise or foolish. After a rough count announce the group's verdict with a blow on a party whistle (or anything makin whizzing noise) for a wise answer, or a honk on a bicycle hooter for a foolish one. This devic could be called the 'Wisdometer'.

You can run the vox pops as a 'live' sketch, or a pre-recorded audio tape, or by making your own video. Get hold of a camcorder or tape recorder, a few group members and go down your local shops and interview the *People on the Pavement* you meet there. You need two or three passers-by to answer each of the questions. It is surprisingly easy and quick to do—anc the young people in your group will be dumbfounded that you've made the tape yourselves.

The questions that you need to ask the *People on the Pavement* for the ten meetings are:

1 *What is the most important thing you can do in life?*
2 *What should you do if you want to become wise?*
3 *What is a fool?*
4 *Complete the sentence, 'Whenever you possibly can . . .'*
5 *What does it mean to be loyal?*
6 *What do you think most affects the way a person behaves?*
7 *How should children treat those who are bringing them up?*
8 *How much responsibility should you take for the consequences of what you say?*
9 *What traps in life are there for people to fall into?*
10 *What do you think it means to trust in God?*

Message in a bottle

Bottled proverb
2 mins

This regular feature focuses on the proverb of the week and aims to give the group a feel for the wisdom and antiquity of the proverb by extracting it from an ancient bottle. (Echoes of the Dead Sea Scrolls.) Each week switch on the ancient Bottled Wisdom music on the audio cassette (see page 125), dim the lights and unveil the wisdom bottle. Then ask for a volunteer to open it, remove the fragment of ancient manuscript and read what it says to the group.

To run this feature get hold of an old bottle from a junk or antique shop. Alternatively take a wine bottle and antiquify it using glue, mud, wax and sand. To make the manuscript stain some white paper with tea, scrumple it up and then flatten it out again, tear the edges and let it dry. (It's worth doing ten pieces all at once.) Write out the week's word of wisdom on one of the bits of antiquated paper, roll it up, tie some cotton round it and pop it in the bottle.

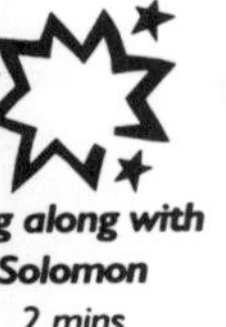

MC Solomon Song

g along with Solomon
2 mins

As King Solomon is famed for his wise words in the book of Proverbs the *Rise Up, Wise Up* meetings wouldn't be complete without an appearance from the great man himself. But we suggest you take a few liberties with his appearance and character. Dress MC Solomon in a shell suit and trainers, with any flash jewellery you can knock up: rings, necklace, shades and crown. Each week he leads the group through his very own *Rise Up, Wise Up* song. It is an American Army style chant in which the group members echo what MC Solomon chants (shouts). Each week a new couplet is added to the song making it longer and longer as the series goes on. The aim of the song is to sum up the point of each meeting in a flash. There is a backing beat for you to use on the *Rise Up, Wise Up* audio cassette (see page 125). An alternative (and shorter) way to do the song is to put the words up on an overhead projector and get MC Solomon to chant the first line of each couplet and the group to reply with the second.

The MC Solomon song

If you want to be real wise
There's something you must realize:
Proverbs shows you what to do
But the rest is up to you.

1. *Seek God's wisdom every day*
And you will learn to walk his way.

2. *Wisdom will be your reward*
If you have reverence for the Lord.

3. *You will go the foolish way*
If you ignore what Proverbs say.

4. *If you can help someone today*
Do it now, please don't delay.

5. *Here is how to be a good friend:*
Be loyal and faithful to the end.

6. *Watch what goes on in your head:*
By your thoughts your life is led.

7. *Your folks are God's guide for you*
So listen to their point of view.

8. *What you say can heal or hurt*
So think twice before you blurt.

9. *If about your life you care*
Stay away from trap and snare.

10. *There's one final thing to say:*
Trust in God come what may.

Activities

Pearls of wisdom

...ndering the proverbs
3 mins

Each of the proverbs you will be exploring in *Rise Up, Wise Up* are genuine 'pearls of wisdom' that should be treasured. To help your group members value and remember them give them each a little bead or 'pearl' to represent the week's proverb and get them to string these on a shoe lace, leather thong or copper wire. Each week you can run through the beads and say together the proverb they represent. Then by the end of the series they should have easily memorised the ten pearls of wisdom. When saying the proverb together I suggest you use the shortened versions below:

- *Look for wisdom as hard as you would for silver or hidden treasure.*
- *To have wisdom you must have reverence for the Lord.*
- *Wisdom is calling out, 'Foolish people! I will give you good advice'.*
- *Whenever you possibly can, do good to those who need it.*
- *Never let go of loyalty and faithfulness.*
- *Be careful how you think: your life is shaped by your thoughts.*
- *Wise children make their parents proud of them.*
- *You will have to live with the consequences of everything you say.*
- *If you love your life, stay away from the traps along the way.*
- *Trust in the Lord with all your heart.*

You can buy coloured beads from craft shops but if you have a large group this will cost a small fortune. A cheaper way to acquire beads would be to go to a jumble sale or junk shop and buy up lots of old bead necklaces and use the beads on them. But make sure the beads on the necklaces you buy are *threaded* not fused. Another cheap source of ideal beads is the long strings of beads sold as Christmas tree decorations. If you think your group would prefer something a bit more 'alternative' then get them threading anything small with a hole in it: bolts, washers, polos, paper clips, old keys, etc. I suggest you collect the strings of beads in at the end of the session so they don't disappear for good before the next meeting.

Bottled prayers

Praying together
3 mins

The *Rise Up, Wise Up* prayer times revolve round getting the group to write prayers on slips of paper and then bottling them in the prayer bottle (any largish plastic bottle will do). Pass the prayer bottle round the group and explain that when it gets to them that is their opportunity to pray their prayer, either silently or out loud, and then bottle it. Having a structure to group prayer times really helped give our group the confidence to pray together.

Planning your meeting

Each *Lightning Bolts* meeting plan contains a selection of activities and ideas for you to take and adapt in the light of your own group's needs. Here are some suggestions on how to plan each meeting.

- Read through the leader's information and all the material.
- Make sure that you are clear about your aim.
- Select only those suggestions and activities that are appropriate for your leaders and group.
- Add your own ideas and worship to create your own style of meeting. Each *Lightning Bolts* meeting plan is a starting point on which you can build. Please feel free to adapt it as much as necessary.

Daily readings

Each of the titles in *Lightning Bolts* is accompanied by ten weeks of daily Bible readings for eleven to fourteen-year-olds. These take the reader all the way through the appropriate book of the Bible or explore selected Bible passages using an amusing and hands-on approach to strike home their message. Do encourage your group members to use them. They will help them get stuck into Bible reading and reinforce all that you are doing in your weekly meetings. On page 127 there is an information sheet about the *Rise Up, Wise Up* readings which you can photocopy and give to the group members to give to their parents. Parents are more likely to buy the readings for their children than the young people are to buy them for themselves!

Audio cassette

An audio cassette is available to accompany *Rise Up, Wise Up*. It contains all the sound effects and theme tunes that you need to run this course. See page 125 for details.

Photocopiable material

The following material from *Rise Up, Wise Up* can be photocopied for use with your group:

- The fools' gallery on page 43.
- The eight fool mug shots on pages 47-54.
- The two proportional 'anatomy of loyalty' diagrams on pages 70 & 71.
- The Loyalty Proverbs worksheets on page 74.
- The 'So just how loyal are you?' self assessment quiz sheet on page 76.
- The four illustrations to the 'Speech-way Code' presentation on pages 97-100.
- The 'Quotes & Consequences' cards on page 103.
- The mouse trap pictures on page 113.
- The 'So just how much do you trust God?' self assessment quiz on pages 120 and 121.
- The Daily Readings information sheet for parents on page 127.

The Quest for Wisdom

The Aim: To understand that seeking the God-given gift of wisdom is the most important thing you can do.

The Lightning Bolt: 'Look for wisdom as hard as you would for silver or some hidden treasure. If you do, you will know what it means to fear the Lord and you will succeed in learning about God. It is the Lord who gives wisdom; from him come knowledge and understanding.' Proverbs 2:4-6

Equipment Check List

PRESENTATIONS
- ❑ theme music
- ❑ sound effects for Solomon story
- ❑ 'P on P' tape or video & Wisdometer
- ❑ wisdom bottle and music
- ❑ Poet's Corner stool & lamp
- ❑ old lady kit & chair
- ❑ MC Solomon outfit & music

ACTIVITIES
- ❑ props for lightning sketches
- ❑ proverb slips
- ❑ interview role play slips
- ❑ prayer bottle, paper & pens
- ❑ shoe laces & beads
- ❑ copies of daily readings

etter to leaders

At first sight today's proverb seems to offer conflicting advice on how to become wise. Is wisdom a God-given gift or a treasure we have to seek out with the determination of a gold digger? If we lay out the proverb a little differently we see that the second leads to the first:
If... *you look for wisdom as hard as you would for silver or some hidden treasure*
Then... *you will know what it means to fear the Lord and succeed in learning about God*
Because... *it is the Lord who gives wisdom; from him come knowledge and understanding.*

The sage says that if we want to know what it means to fear the Lord and learn about God we have to rise up and start seeking wisdom with real determination. Fortunately we don't have to go on our quest in the dark: he is our guide and the book of Proverbs our guide book. But we certainly can't just sit at home and wait for wisdom to arrive in the post. We have to get out there and get looking, praying and thinking. Then we will not ***'find'*** wisdom ourselves, rather God will ***give*** it to us because he is the ultimate source of all true wisdom.

- ***How much do you want to know what it means to fear the Lord and succeed in learning about God?***
- ***Why not make your youth group's quest through Proverbs part of your own personal quest for wisdom? Why not talk to God about it now?***

Presentations

Welcome and introduction

Sparking off
1 min

Have the *Rise Up, Wise Up* theme music playing as the group arrives and give them all a very warm welcome. Introduce *Rise Up, Wise Up* by explaining that over the coming weeks you w be taking a look at some power packed proverbs that will help you all to rise up and wise up

The man behind the wisdom

A story
4 mins

King Solomon was the main man behind the book of Proverbs and his wisdom is legendary. introduce the group to Solomon read the following enhanced account of his path to power a request for wisdom, based on 1 Kings 3, 10 & 11. The sound effects can be found on the *Ri Up, Wise Up* audio cassette (see page 125 for details). There is a one-second gap between each sound effect on the tape, so simply press the pause button on the tape machine after ea effect and release it again when it is time for the next one.

King Solomon of Israel was one of the greatest kings that ever reigned on planet earth: **(TRUMPET FANFARE)** *awesome, impressive, overpowering* (**MASSIVE GONG SOUNI** *Under his reign the Kingdom of Israel became richer, stronger, more powerful than it had ever be before.*

King Solomon lived in oriental splendour: **(ROYAL ORIENTAL MUSIC playing in the background as you read the following description of his palace)** *He built himself a palace the like of which the world had never seen. Magnificent buildings set in hanging gardens, fu of bubbling fountains, exotic plants, peacocks and monkeys. His palace was a succession of splen halls, majestic colonnades, and royal rooms: royal bedrooms, royal bathing rooms, royal hair salor royal gymnasiums, royal dining halls, royal room after royal room, all adorned with sumptuous red and gold and decorated with exquisite tapestries and sculptures. The cool marble corridors echoe with the crisp footsteps of his many servants and the elegant strains of the King's personal orchestra. King Solomon lived in style: he sat on gold, he slept on gold, he ate off gold, he dressed gold.*

One of the King's many talents was for business **(CASH TILL)**. *His international export and import trade boomed. Over land he had numerous camel trains travelling to far countries over barren deserts and returning with incense and spices, gold, and precious stones, the like of which one had seen before* **(GASP)**. *He not only had total control of the land corridors but he also monopolised the shipping lanes: his Phoenician ships traded in smelted ore and returned with cargoes of silver, hardwood, jewels, ivory, monkeys, chariots and horses.*

Solomon was also a great politician. One of the first things he did as king was marry the Pharaoh Egypt's daughter **(HERE COMES THE BRIDE TUNE)**. *A cunning move. The neighbouring Egyptians were now relatives not enemies (and came over for tea not a blood bath). Solomon pursued this 'make up and marry' policy with all his potentially hostile neighbours* **(HERE COM THE BRIDE TUNE)**, *and by and large his 40 year reign was peaceful, even if he did have ove 700 wives to keep happy.*

Rumours of King Solomon's vast wealth, immense power, and great kingly authority spread far and wide - even as far as the land of Sheba **(ARABIAN MUSIC)**, *and so astonished the Queen th*

she made the extremely long and perilous journey to meet Solomon herself. She was astonished to find that King Solomon's wisdom was far greater even than she had heard. King Solomon was awesome (**MASSIVE GONG SOUND)**.

But Solomon hadn't always been a king. Once he had been a baby: the child of King David **(BABY CRYING)**. *He became king in his early twenties and a mighty big task he had ahead of him. His dad had been Mr Popular with his people - they loved him dearly and were devoted to him. Now the young Solomon had to stand in his father's shoes with his crown on his head and rule his vast kingdom. A daunting prospect* **(SUSPENSE CHORDS)**. *That's the problem with having a famous dad.*

Well, soon after Solomon became king God spoke to him in a big religious meeting. In a vision God asked Solomon what he could do to help. Solomon thought about it and then said that he was very aware of the big job he had ahead of him and would really appreciate it if God would give him wisdom and the ability to know right and wrong. This pleased God **(MASSIVE APPLAUSE)** *and he promised Solomon that he would give him wisdom abundantly - so abundantly that he would be the wisest man alive. And what's more he'd throw in prosperity, power, peace and long life as well.*

From that day on King Solomon was known as Mr Wise. God gave him real insight into the way people's minds worked: take the case of the two very distressed women who came to him one day to settle a dispute. They shared a house and had both just given birth to baby boys. One night one of them woke to find her baby had died so she swapped the babies round while the other mother slept. When the other mum woke she noticed that her 'dead' baby was not her baby at all. They came to Solomon to get it sorted out. King Solomon listened, then instructed his servant to cut the living baby in two and give half to each **(SUSPENSE CHORDS)**. *At this the real mother begged Solomon not to do it, but to let the other woman have the child, whilst the dead child's mother willingly agreed for the child to be cut in two. So of course the wise king knew who the true mother was, and gave the child to her.*

Over the years the wisdom of King Solomon became legendary. His wise words were recorded, collected and included in books of short sayings or proverbs. These wisdom collections became indispensable reading matter to all who wanted to rise up and wise up. Over the last 3,000 years they have been translated into countless different languages and studied all over the world. Many of Solomon's proverbs are recorded in the Bible - the world's best selling book. If you open your Bible near the middle you will find The Book of Proverbs - a collection of ancient wise sayings, many spoken by Solomon, and collected together as a wise living manual for future generations. The astounding wisdom of the awesome King Solomon **(MASSIVE GONG SOUND)** *has spanned the centuries and is ready to help us rise up and wise up now.*

THE GREAT WISDOM QUEST

The People on the Pavement

Street wise?
2 mins

Tell the group that you are going to start King Solomon's *Rise Up, Wise Up* course by explori what is the most important thing we can do in life. Go on to explain that you have been out and about on the streets of your town finding out the views of the *People on the Pavement*. (page 20.) You asked them what they thought was the most important thing you can do in life and this is what they said... Play the interviews on your audio cassette or your own home m video. After each answer pause the tape or video and ask the group to vote by a show of hands on whether the person on the pavement was being wise or foolish. After a rough cou announce the group's verdict with a blow on a party whistle for a wise answer, or a honk o the bicycle hooter for a foolish one. From now on I'll refer to these two noises as the 'Wisdometer'.

Message in a bottle

Bottled proverb
2 mins

Play the atmospheric wisdom bottle backing track on the audio cassette and produce the ancient wisdom bottle (see page 21). Explain that it contains a very old manuscript written by King Solomon himself. Ask for a volunteer to open it, fish out the ancient manuscript and read the words of wisdom. The words of wisdom found in the bottle this week are as follows: *'Look for wisdom as hard as you would for silver or some hidden treasure. If you do, you will know what it means to fear the Lord and you will succeed in learning about God. It is the Lord who gives wisdom; from him come knowledge and understanding.'*

Eric the armadillo

…et's corner
3 mins

Set up a stool in the middle of the room, dim the lights, switch on an angle-poise lamp and point it at the stool. Then introduce this week's guest on 'Poet's Corner' and ask them to read this poem about an armadillo called Eric who goes on a quest to become wise. Read the poem with as much drama as you can and get another leader (or the group) to interrupt with the ***'To be what?'*** lines printed in bold.

I wonder what it really is you'd like to do in life?
To be wealthy, to be famous, to be or get a wife?
Well, I had a four-legged friend who took me by surprise;
Eric the armadillo really wanted to be wise!
So when he was a youngster he did what his mother said;
He went to school and worked so hard: he thought, he wrote, he read.
And after years of studying and being called a swot,
He got straight 'A's in all exams; but wiser he was not.

He wanted to be wise.
To be what?
To be wise!
I know it's a surprise,
But still he wasn't wise.

So Eric started snuffling for a different wisdom scent,
And waddling on his wisdom quest on his way he went.
He toured the streets of youth-ville and could not believe his eyes.
'At last', he cried, 'I've found it! I have to be ***street wise***!'
He learnt the slang for all the drugs; jellies, Es and eggs.
He got the suss on 'right on' dress, for head, tail, shell and legs.
He knew the names of all the bands and just which one was what,
But even though he now was cool, much wiser he was not!

He wanted to be wise.
To be what?
To be wise!
He tried to improvise,
But still he wasn't wise.

Eric didn't back into his armour-plated shell;
He followed the next wisdom scent that his snout could smell.
He waddled down the city streets through zones of enterprise,
And suddenly saw the pressing need to be ***worldly wise***.
He bought himself a lovely house, and got it all insured.
He fixed a decent pension so his future was secured.
He started saving hard-earned cash and built up quite a lot,
But deep down in his heart he knew that wiser he was not.

He wanted to be wise.
To be what?
To be wise!
He tried enterprise,
But still he wasn't wise.

Eric was now flummoxed so he thought for quite a while,
And as it dawned on him he gave an armadillo smile.
He'd racked his brain for wisdom 'types' and come up with the 'sage'.
Yes, he'd be wise if he could get the ***wisdom of old age***.
He bought himself a long white beard, and powder for his hair,
He moved into a hermit's cave with an old rocking chair
But all that heavy thinking just fuzzed his brain somewhat,
And as he waddled home he knew that wiser he was not.

He wanted to be wise.
To be what?
To be wise!
You may empathize,
But still he wasn't wise.

Poor Eric was now panicked that he'd never find the way,
So in deepest desperation he began to pray.
Then God explained to him that he had been a fool
To think that wisdom was about being clever, rich or cool;
For wisdom is a free gift that God alone can give
He gives it to all who seek him so they can wisely live.
At this blinding revelation of how wisdom should be got
Eric prayed for wisdom and hit wisdom's top jackpot.

Famous last words

e benefits of wisdom
2 mins

Dress a leader as an old person, sit them in an arm chair and get them to say the following words paraphrased from Proverbs 2 to the group as if they were their famous last words:

'Listen my dears. I've got something very important I want to say to you. If you want to learn how to live intelligently and how to be honest, just and fair; if you want to become wise and learn how to be resourceful; then listen to the wise words of MC Solomon from the book of Proverbs. Learn what he teaches you and never forget what he tells you to do. Listen to what is wise and try to understand it. Yes, beg for knowledge; plead for insight. Look for it as hard as you would for silver or some hidden treasure. If you do, you will know what it means to fear the Lord and you will succeed in learning about God. It is the Lord who gives wisdom; from him come knowledge and understanding. If you listen to God, you will know what is right, just and fair. You will know what you should do. You will become wise, and your knowledge will give you pleasure. Your insight and understanding will protect you and prevent you from doing the wrong thing. (She then dozes off.)

MC Solomon song

g along with Solomon
2 mins

Introduce the group to MC Solomon who struts in wearing his shell suit, flash gear, rings, necklace, shades and crown and takes the group through the first few lines of his song. The group repeats each line after MC Solomon and the backing beat is on the audio cassette. Here is the introductory verse and this week's couplet.

If you want to be real wise
There's something you must realize:
Proverbs shows you what to do
But the rest is up to you.

Seek God's wisdom every day
And you will learn to walk his way

Activities

Welcome back

Chit chat
4 mins

Welcome everyone back to the group and give them a chance to chat together. This is important and will help everyone to relax and catch up on each other's news. Take this opportunity to talk to individuals in the group.

The choice is yours

ne wish . . .
3 mins

Ask the group members what they would wish for if God appeared to them in a dream and asked them what they would like him to do for them (as he did to Solomon). Get each person to write their wish anonymously on a piece of paper and put it in a hat in the middle of the room. Then pass the hat round and get each person to pick one of the 'wish' slips of paper and as a group try and work out whose wish is whose. If appropriate go on to discuss their wish and the wish of Solomon.

Quests of life

Lightning sketches
12 mins

Split into smaller groups and ask each to prepare a sketch in which someone goes on a determined quest for either fame, fortune, treasure, success, or love, etc. To help stimulate their imaginations give them a few random objects to work into their sketches (e.g. walking stick, radio and tube of glue). After eight minutes or so get back together and perform them each other. Perhaps you could then discuss which of the quests was the most worthwhile.

Sorting out the proverb

Pondering the proverb
5 mins

Divide the proverb into as many sections as you have group members. For a group of eight members you might divide it like this:

- *Look for wisdom as hard*
- *as you would for silver or*
- *some hidden treasure. If you do*
- *you will know what it means to*
- *fear the Lord and you will succeed*
- *in learning about God. It is*
- *the Lord who gives wisdom; from*
- *him come knowledge and understanding.*

Hand each person one section written on a slip of paper. They are not to show their slip to anyone but have to say it out loud over and over again and sort themselves into the correct order. When they think they have done this get them each to say their phrase in turn and se they are right.

Interviews

Role plays
5 mins

Split the group into pairs. Ask the group members to imagine that they have applied for the 'award' of God's wisdom (as if it was some kind of grant or fund). Split the group into pairs a hand one member of each pair a copy of the list of interview questions (below), and the oth member one of the following 'character' slips. Ask them to do a role play in which the interviewer interviews the applicant using some of the suggested questions and the applicant to respond in keeping with the description on their character slip. After a couple of minutes swap over or perform the role plays to the whole group.

INTERVIEW QUESTIONS
- *Why do you want the award of God's wisdom?*
- *What do you think God's wisdom is?*
- *What difference will it make to your life?*
- *What would you do if you didn't get the award?*
- *Why do you think we should give the award to you?*
- *How do we know you will use the award wisely?*

CHARACTER SLIPS

- **Wendy or Walter Wise:** *Very keen to receive God's wisdom. It really is the thing s/he wants most in life.*
- **Andy or Alison Apathy:** *Really can't be bothered. Didn't want to apply for the award - his/her mum filled in the form for him/her. Can't wait to get home.*
- **Nick or Nicola Nervous:** *Would very much like to be given the award but is worried that s/he doesn't deserve it and that perhaps it would be wasted on him/her.*
- **Adrian or Amanda Arrogant:** *Applied for the award because it's good for the career, but doesn't really think s/he needs Gods wisdom that much. Feels pretty wise already.*
- **Dave or Diana Desperate:** *Has a natural talent for making silly mistakes and desperately needs God's wisdom to help him/her survive.*

Conclude by making the point that with God's wisdom there is not just one successful applicant; we can all receive it. However, we have to really want it and actively seek it because it won't just land on our plate.

Bottled prayers

Praying together
3 mins

Hand out slips of paper and pens and encourage each group member to write a letter to God asking him to help them become wise. Pass round the prayer bottle (see page 23) so that when it gets to each person they can pray their prayer either out loud or silently and then bottle it.

Pearls of wisdom

…dering the proverbs
3 mins

The proverbs we are looking at in *Rise Up, Wise Up* are like pearls of wisdom to be treasured. To help the group remember them, hand each group member a length of copper wire (20cm) or a shoe lace and explain that over the term you will be stringing beads (pearls of wisdom) on them. Each bead represents one of the proverbs. (See page 23.) Hand out the first of the ten beads and ask them to thread it on their wire; this represents proverb number one: *'Look for wisdom as hard as you would for silver or hidden treasure.'* Get every one to hold bead number one and say the proverb together a couple of times. (Each week you will work through the beads, and say each proverb in turn.) I suggest you collect the strings of beads in at the end of each session and look after them till the next meeting.

A proverb a day

…aily notes
2 mins

Hand out some copies of the *Rise Up, Wise Up* Daily Bible Notes or photocopies of the information sheet for parents on page 127. Encourage the group members to buy a copy of the notes and give them a try. They explore a proverb a day for seventy days and aim to help the reader learn the way of wisdom.

Wisdom's Main Ingredient

2

The Aim: To see that to be truly wise you have to have reverence for God.

The Lightning Bolt: 'To have [wisdom], you must first have reverence for the Lord.' Proverbs 1:7

Equipment Check List

PRESENTATIONS
❑ theme music
❑ 'P on P' tape or video & Wisdometer
❑ wisdom bottle and music
❑ beginner's tour of God props & music
❑ head-to-head table & chairs
❑ MC Solomon outfit & music

ACTIVITIES
❑ 10 famous people pics
❑ tape recorder & blank tape
❑ paper & pens
❑ prayer bottle, paper & pens
❑ shoe laces & beads
❑ copies of daily readings

Letter to leaders

Imagine how you would feel if you were given the opportunity to spend a day with a person for whom you had great respect; perhaps a football star, or great musician. No doubt your reverence for them would make you humble in their presence, and willing to learn from their instruction. In their company you would become a wiser footballer or musician. That is the point behind this proverb. Reverence makes us humble, teachable and open. Reverence for God makes us humble, teachable and open to him. Wise in other words.

The problem is that though we may know that X is a great footballer because we see them play and know all about them, it is not so easy to get a hold on the awesome reality of God. I one thing knowing in our heads that God is the almighty, majestic ruler of the universe but qui another to let that knowledge sink into our hearts and become a knowledge ***of*** him. If that is t happen we have to go out of our way to find out all we can about God and let what we discover and he reveals sink deep into our lives.

- ***Stop for a minute and think about God. Perhaps you could make a list of words that describe him and then meditate on each one. Ask God to help you understa more fully who he really is.***

- ***Why not invest in a copy of* Knowing God *by J.I. Packer and actively go on a ques to get to know God better? Reverence and wisdom will follow on naturally.***

resentations

Welcome and introduction

rking off
min

Have the *Rise Up, Wise Up* theme music playing as the group arrives and give them all a very warm welcome. Introduce the series and explain that in the coming weeks you will be taking a look at some power-packed proverbs that will help you all to wise up. Go on to say that the subject of today's meeting is 'wisdom's main ingredient'; in other words what you should do if you want to become wise—which is exactly what you asked the People on the Pavement...

The People on the Pavement

et wise?
mins

Explain that you have been out and about on the streets of your town canvassing the views of the *People on the Pavement*. You asked them what they thought you should do if you want to become wise and this is what they said... Play the recorded interviews on your audio cassette or home made video. After each answer let the group vote on whether the person on the pavement was being wise or foolish, and announce the verdict using the two sound effects of the Wisdometer.

Message in a bottle

ottled
roverb
mins

Switch on the wisdom bottle backing track on the audio cassette and produce the wisdom bottle. Explain what it is and ask for a volunteer to open it, remove the ancient manuscript and read Solomon's words of wisdom to the group. The text on this week's manuscript is, *'To have wisdom, you must first have reverence for the Lord.'*

Word of the week

cinating
ts about
verence
1 min

This is a very short feature focusing on the word 'reverence'. Jump up and with colossal enthusiasm and 'racing-commentator' speed run through the following facts about the word 'Reverence':

Word of the Week: REVERENCE!

- *Did you know that 'Reverence' is a nine letter word beginning with R and ending in everence!*
- *Did you know that 'Reverence' is a feeling or attitude of profound respect usually reserved for God!*
- *Did you know that there are three words beginning with D that mean the exact opposite of Reverence! They are Despise, Dishonour, and Disrespect.*
- *And lastly did you know that the word 'Reverence' rhymes with magnificence, omniscience, omnipotence, omnipresence, transcendence and self-existence! All words that describe God and are reasons for having reverence for him.*

The beginner's tour of God

A guided tour
4 mins

This feature takes the group on a tour of the key truths that we know about God as reveale the Bible, and aims to make it clear why it is wise to revere God. Before the meeting write the words SPIRIT, INFINITE, ETERNAL, UNCHANGEABLE, WISDOM, POWER, HOLINESS, JUSTICE, GOODNESS and TRUTH on separate pieces of paper in large writir Pin or stick them to the walls and ceiling of the meeting room. Get hold of a powerful torch (preferably with a narrow beam) and make the room as dark as possible. Take the group on *The Beginner's Tour of God* using the following tour guide script. To make matters easier the script could be read by one leader while another points out the features with the torch. The tour is based on a guided tour of some caves I once went to. Play the cave sound effects on the audio cassette as you run the tour.

Tour Guide: Ladies and gentlemen, welcome to *The Beginner's Tour of God*. You have inde made a wise choice to spend the next few minutes delving into the highest science, the lofti contemplation, the mightiest philosophy that can ever occupy the human mind: yes, the nat of God Almighty.

Before we begin our tour I must warn you that God is a subject so vast that all our thoughts will be lost in his hugeness; he is a subject so deep that our pride will be drowned in his infin Be warned, ladies and gentlemen, that your tiny human brain will be out of its depth when i contemplates God. Few people emerge from the shortest *Beginner's Tour of God* without be humbled. But as well as humbling the mind *The Beginner's Tour of God* will also expand it. It h been said that a serious investigation into the subject of God is the most powerful mind-expanding experience known to humankind. So, ladies and gentlemen, please pluck up your courage and step out with me on *The Beginner's Tour of God*.

The first stop on our tour is the *Westminster Shorter Catechism* which gives us what was onc described as 'the best definition of God ever written'. It answers the question 'What is God? explaining that *'God is a Spirit, infinite, eternal, and unchangeable in His being, wisdom, power, holiness, justice, goodness, and truth.'* Don't worry if you didn't get all that because as our tou progresses we will take a glimpse at each of these astonishing truths about God. I will point them out with the aid of this torch.

(Point to the word ***SPIRIT*** *with the torch)* Ladies and gentlemen, if you follow the beam of m torch you will see high above your heads that God is a ***Spirit*** *(Gasp)*. He is pure spirit with r form or parts, and for that reason he has no physical presence. You cannot see him. This do not mean that God is a vague 'thing'. No, God is a personal spirit: he is a rational, thinking character.

(Point to the word ***INFINITE*** *with the torch)* Slightly down to the left you will see that God is ***infinite*** Spirit *(Gasp)*. Here we pass completely out of the reach of our limited human experience. We human beings are caught within the confines of time and space *(State curren time, date and place)*. And our knowledge and experience are limited also. But God is infinit spirit, which means that he is absolutely unlimited in all aspects of his being *(Gasp)*. Excuse m madam, if you're feeling faint please do take a seat. He is also infinite in space, which means he is absolutely everywhere at once. He is in every single atom.

(ETERNAL) Now if you look high up to the left, you will see that God is ***eternal*** *(Gasp)*. C is eternal Spirit. This means that he is infinite in time; he has always existed and will always e: There is no 'before' or 'after' with God *(Gasp)*.

(UNCHANGEABLE) Now ladies and gentlemen, if you look slightly down to the right, you will see that God is ***unchangeable*** *(Gasp)*. God is unchangeable Spirit. He is always consistent. He does not change. He is the same yesterday, today, forever. He is not like you and me who change as we get older, or with our moods. God can always be relied upon to be the same. Quite extraordinary!

(WISDOM) Now, if you follow the beam of my torch round and up you will see that God is infinite in his ***wisdom*** *(Gasp)*. There is nothing he does not know, he understands everything.

(POWER) Over here we see that God is infinite in his ***power***; he is all-powerful *(Gasp)*. Nothing is too hard for him. Could someone please give that gentleman a glass of water. Thank you.

(HOLINESS) Further up we see that he is infinite and unchanging in his ***holiness***. This means that he is separate from all other beings. He is the only one who is God. He is different from the things he has created. And he is separate from all that is evil *(Gasp)*.

Ladies and gentlemen, I can see that you are beginning to feel the humbling and mind-expanding effects of *The Beginners Tour of God*, so I think I'd better start to draw the tour to a close. But before I do let me just point out three other important features of God. *(Point out the words **JUSTICE, GOODNESS & TRUTH** with the torch.)* As you can clearly see God is also infinite and unchanging in his Justice, in his Goodness and in his Truth. Maybe you will be able to investigate those extraordinary qualities further next time you take *The Beginner's Tour of God.*

(With emotion) Ladies and gentlemen, it is always a great honour and indeed a humbling experience taking people on *The Beginner's Tour of God*. Each time I am astonished and awe-struck by the sheer Godness of God. I am overwhelmed by his holiness and greatness and the way in which he wants to be a friend and father to each one of us. Of course what we have glimpsed today is just the tiniest fraction of his being, but what a privilege it is to see even that. Ladies and gentlemen, may you all go on to know and revere our God more each day. Thank you very much. God bless you.

But why should I respect God?
Well, he's bigger than you for a start.

Head-to-head

A discussion
2 mins

Hold a head-to-head conversation in which two characters face each other over a table and hold a conversation along the following lines. One enthusiastically expands on the awesomeness of God, but the other, though agreeing that God is omnipotent, etc., can't see how it's relevant to him/her. The point the sketch makes is that to be truly wise your reverence for God should lead you to be obedient to his ways.

A You know, I've been thinking about God.

B Yeah, yeah, God, mmmm.

A You know God… He's quite amazing, quite amazing!

B *(nodding vigorously)* Oh, I know. Quite amazing.

A Did you know—now this really is mind-blowing—did you know that God is 'self-existent'?

B Oh, yes, self-existent! Amazing in'it!

A It's absolutely mind-blowingly-incredibly-astonishing. He is self-existent! Phewee!

B … err, you know 'self-existent' … err what does it mean?

A It means that God exists totally independently of everything else in the universe. You and I and everything else depend on him for our existence, but God is not dependent on anything!

B Oh, yeah!

A Well, don't you think that's amazing?

B Well, it's OK…

A OK? Just OK? *(pause)* Well did you know that God is... did you know God is 'all-powerful'? Now that really is amazing. You've got to admit it, mate!

B *(unenthusiastically)* Yeah, that is amazing. Got to admit it—that is amazing.

A Well, you don't sound amazed. Look, I'm saying that God is 'all-powerful'! That means he can do anything. Absolutely anything! Nothing's too hard for him! If he wanted to he could make *(your local football team)* win the Club Championship! He could make the world spin twice as fast, he can do anything!

B Yeah, yeah.

A And you know what's more; God—this bit always brings a lump to my throat—God, well, he loves us. He loves us little human beings.

B Oh, he does, he does!

A It's incredible isn't it that the almighty creator of the universe actually loves us puny, sinful, twisted human beings. Don't you think that's just mind-boggling?

B Truly mind-blowing!

A So you agree with me that God is all-powerful, he is self-existent, he's absolutely mind-blowingly awesome and what is more that he loves us?

B *(nodding)* Oh, yeah, I agree, I agree.

A Well, what difference is it going to make to your life?

B Difference?… None I suppose. He's there and I'm here and we don't bother each other. Know what I mean?

A But that's impossible! You can't believe that God is God and not let it make a differen
Listen mate, he deserves your respect.

B Oh, but I do respect him, he's a good bloke.

A But it's got to be more than that. Your respect for him should mean that you try and what he wants you to. Your respect should lead to ACTION. *(bangs table)*

B Yeah, yeah! *(looks at watch)* Look mate, I can't hang around here all day, I've got to g to the University. I'm doing a course to make me clever. I can see you're impressed!

A You still haven't understood, have you? You can have as many degrees as you like, bu you don't have respect for God, you're a fool.

B How dare you! Do you realize I've got more exams than you. Call me a fool will ya!

A Being wise isn't about exams, mate. It's about respecting God, doing things his way: ' have wisdom, you must first have reverence for the Lord.'

B Well, I've got plenty of that mate, as I've tried to explain, but you just don't seem to understand. See ya.

A *(shakes his head sadly)*

MC Solomon song

Sing along with Solomon
2 mins

Enter MC Solomon who takes the group through the first few lines of his song. Play the back beat on the audio cassette and run through the song so far, finishing with this week's couplet, which is as follows:

Wisdom will be your reward
If you have reverence for the Lord.

Activities

To revere or not to revere

Ranking ten personalities
5 mins

Before the meeting look through some young people's magazines or newspapers and cut ou photographs of a range of contemporary characters that the group members will know, e.g. politicians, film and sports stars, cartoon characters, TV presenters, etc. Stick each of these photos onto a separate card. Alternatively just write their names on separate slips of paper. Spread these out on the floor in front of the group and ask them to rank them in order of hc much they respect or revere them. If at all possible try and get the group to come to an agre group decision. Go on to discuss why they do or don't revere the ten different characters. Tr and draw out any recurring themes.

A 24hr message

Recording messages
15 mins

Split the group into pairs or threes and ask them to read the proverb together and then compose a message to go on MC Solomon's Rise Up, Wise Up 24hr telephone help line. Tl message should explain the first simple steps to becoming wise. Perhaps it could start like this *'Thank you for calling MC Solomon's Rise Up, Wise Up telephone help line. There now follows a short message from his majesty for all who want to rise up and wise up. You have not been charged for this call...'* If possible get hold of a tape recorder and a blank tape and let the group members record their message. Then play them back to each other.

A God alphabet

God words
10 mins

Split the group into pairs or threes, hand them paper and pens, and ask them to write an A to Z of God. For example, A is for almighty, B is for beautiful, C is for compassionate. Once they have had time to compile their masterpiece get back together and read them to each other and discuss. If you have time perhaps you could merge the individual alphabets to produce the group's definitive God alphabet.

Reflections on God

My story
1 min

Tell the group briefly, openly and honestly what you find awesome about God and what you think it means to have reverence for him. This will lead naturally into the prayer time.

Bottled prayers

Praying together
3 mins

Hand everyone a slip of paper and a pen and encourage them to write a tribute to God focusing on one aspect of his nature (see A to Z). Pass round the prayer bottle so that when it gets to each person they can read their tribute either silently or out loud and then bottle it.

Pearls of wisdom

Pondering the proverbs
3 mins

Remind the group that the proverbs we are looking at this term are like pearls of wisdom to be treasured. To help them remember this, hand out bead number two and ask them to thread it on their shoe lace or copper wire; this represents proverb number two, *'To have wisdom, you must first have reverence for the Lord.'* Get everyone to hold bead number two and say the proverb together a couple of times. Then all hold pearl one and run through last week's pearl of wisdom together.

A proverb a day

Daily notes
2 mins

Ask the group how they got on with their daily readings and encourage them to keep going. A little bit of encouragement will go a long way. If there is time perhaps you could all do a reading together.

Wisdom's Warning

The Aim: To warn the group about the danger of becoming a fool.

The Lighting Bolt: 'Listen! Wisdom is calling out... "Foolish people! How l
do you want to be foolish?... Listen when I reprimand you; I will give you good
advice and share my knowledge with you." ' Proverbs 1:20–23

Equipment check List

PRESENTATIONS

- ❑ theme music
- ❑ fools of a feather slips
- ❑ 'P on P' tape or video & Wisdometer
- ❑ wisdom bottle and music
- ❑ mug shots on OHPs & Inspector Wise kit
- ❑ radio phone in kit
- ❑ MC Solomon outfit & music

ACTIVITIES

- ❑ copies of mug shots
- ❑ copies of cartoon strip & pens
- ❑ paper & pens
- ❑ prayer bottle, paper & pens
- ❑ shoe laces & beads
- ❑ copies of daily readings

Letter to leaders

The editor of the book of Proverbs has selected proverbs identifying a very wide-ranging ca list of 'fools' including the *simple*, the *hot head*, the *conceited*, the *sluggard*, the *drunkard*, the *greedy*, the *trouble-maker* and the *gossip-liar*. I have counted over two hundred proverbs de with the varieties of fool and they are all bluntly dismissive. The general gist is that fools will never learn. So why, if fools are such hopeless cases, does the book of Proverbs waste bre going on about them?

The reason must surely be that you don't become a fool overnight. Folly is a slippery slope down which you slowly slither. The book of Proverbs gives us this detailed description of th ways of the fool as a warning to us. We are meant to study both it and our lives carefully to if we are developing any of those foolish traits, and if so take corrective action, and take it fa

- ***Read through the gallery of fools opposite and carefully consider if you might n be starting to slide down any of those foolish slopes.***
- ***If you think you might be what will you do about it? It might be a good idea to the help of a wise friend.***

The Gullibles

A fool will believe anything; sensible people watch their step. 14:15

The Angrys

People with a hot temper do foolish things; wiser people remain calm. 14:17

The Know-it-Alls

Show me a conceited person and I will show you someone who is arrogant, proud, and inconsiderate. 21:24

The Lazys

Lazy people turn over in bed. They get no further than a door swinging on its hinges. 26:14

The Smasheds

Drinking too much makes you loud and foolish. It's stupid to get drunk. 20:1

The Want-Mores

Human desires are like the world of the dead—there is always room for more. 27:20

The Troublemakers

If you are always planning evil, you will earn a reputation as a troublemaker. 24:8

The Gossip-Liars

Gossip is spread by wicked people; they stir up trouble and break up friendships. 16:28

Presentations

Welcome & introduction

Sparking off
1 min

Play the *Rise Up, Wise Up* theme music as the group arrives. Give everyone a warm welcom and introduce the subject of the meeting - the warning wisdom gives us about the dangers o becoming a fool.

Fools of a feather...

Pairing up
5 mins

Hand each person a slip of paper on which is written the name of one of the eight fools belo They must not tell anyone who they are, but on the word of command they are to start acti like their foolish character and try and pair up with other members of the group who are behaving in the same way. After about four minutes they should have formed into eight little foolish clusters. You will make it easier for the less confident members of the group if you pri some leaders and older group members beforehand to each take one of the fool types and really go for it. Shy people can then just join up with them without the embarrassment of having to fool around.

- *Mr Gullible*
- *Ms Angry*
- *Miss Know-it-All*
- *Mr Lazy*
- *Mrs Gossip-Liar*
- *Mr Smashed*
- *Mrs Want-More*
- *Master Trouble-Maker*

The People on the Pavement

Street wise?
2 mins

Play the clip of tape or show the home-video in which two or three People on the Pavemen answer the question, 'What is a fool?' After each answer give the group members the chance to vote on the wisdom or folly of the answer then declare the verdict using the Wisdometer.

Message in a bottle

Bottled proverb
2 mins

Play the wisdom bottle theme music, unveil the wisdom bottle and ask for a volunteer to op it, fish out the ancient manuscript and read the proverb. The message in the bottle this week *'Listen! Wisdom is calling out... "Foolish people! How long do you want to be foolish?... Listen when I reprimand you; I will give you good advice and share my knowledge with you."'*

Foolish mug shots

arning from ector Wise
4 mins

Explain to the group with mock seriousness that you are about to have a visit from an inspector from the FID (Fools Intelligence Department) who has an important warning to give you all. Introduce Inspector Wise, dressed in detective mac and hat. The inspector then explains that s/he has the unpleasant task of warning the group about a series of foolish characters who may try to influence them at various points in their lives. They may even find these characters lurking inside themselves. The inspector explains that s/he is going to show the group eight mug shots of dangerous fools currently at large. S/he asks them to look at the pictures and descriptions very carefully to see if they are familiar. If so, serious action needs to be taken before the situation gets out of hand.

The inspector then displays the eight mug-shots (on pages 47 to 54) on an overhead projector. (Photocopy the artwork onto acetates.) S/he reads out the name, favourite occupation, and motto for life of each one, followed by the word of warning, which is of course the proverb.

Transformed!

phone in
3 min

This is a radio phone-in programme in which a range of people put their views on the subject of foolishness and how to escape from it. This presentation is very straightforward to run. One leader (the Presenter) sits at a desk at the front of the room with headphones and a copy of the script. The characters who phone in simply hold their nose and read their part from 'off stage'. They could even all be read by the same person putting on different voices. Do adapt and extend the script as you see fit. Start and finish the script by playing the local radio jingle on the audio cassette.

Cast: PRESENTER, MR NO-LONGER-SMASHED, MS ANGRY, MR HUMBLE

Presenter Good morning. You're listening to Lightning Bolts radio with (your name). It's five past ten and it's time for our regular phone-in spot. Yes, this is your chance to put your views on the subject of foolishness. If you have anything to say on the warning put out by Inspector Wise, or if you have experience of being foolish, or have any tips on how to avoid folly, please do phone and share them with us. The number to call is 01010 101010. And we have our first caller on the line now; a Mr No-Longer-Smashed from County Sober. Mr No-Longer-Smashed are you there?

Mr N-L-S Yes. My point is this. About ten years ago I went through a bit of a bad patch in my life, and I, er, took to drinking rather too heavily. And, er, a friend who was worried about me sent me on a residential weekend at the MC Solomon Retreat House where the staff helped me to see how foolish I was being, trying to escape from my problems through getting smashed, and slowly they helped me rebuild my life. It wasn't easy, but the point I'm trying to make is that when you are being foolish it is hard to tell sometimes and you need someone to point it out to you and help you wise up.

Presenter Mr No-Longer-Smashed, thank you very much for you call. Our next caller is a Ms Angry from Wrathtown.

Ms Angry Hello. Well, I was phoning for some advice really, because I listened to what Inspector Wise said and I think that I might be a bit of a fool with my temper.

I was wanting some advice on how to wise up. Do you have any suggestions, please?

Presenter Ms Angry, could you just tell us a little bit more about your anger?

Ms Angry Yes, well I don't really mean to get angry. It's just that lots of things annoy m and when I get annoyed I tend to get angry inside and then maybe slam doors and shout at people and even sometimes smash things.

Presenter Ms Angry, if you just stay on the line we'll see if our next caller has any suggestions. A Mr Humble from Meektown, Wales. Hello Mr Humble.

Mr Humble Hello. I wanted to tell you how helpful I have found MC Solomon's *Rise Up Wise Up* course. It really has changed my life. Before I started the course I was a bit of a know-it-all and must have been a complete pain in the neck t everyone I met. Well, MC Solomon gave me a glimpse of how awesome God is, and that really helped me see myself as I really am. It knocked the arrogance out of me. So I'd just really like to commend MC Solomon's wisdom course to everyone whether they are foolish or not.

Presenter Thank you so much for sharing that, Mr Humble. Now do you have any tip you could give Ms Angry?

Mr Humble Well, I'm not sure if this will help, but I found that it made a big difference when I went and talked to God. He really helped me see my life in perspective. If you see things his way, Ms Angry, I don't think you'll get so annoyed. And of course it is OK to really shout at God if you're angry with him. He can take it. The other thing to try next time you start getting angry is counting to ten before you do or say anything. If you are a bit like a bomb with a short fuse, anything that makes the fuse longer will help.

Presenter Ms Angry, was that at all helpful?

Ms Angry Oh yes, I think so, I'll try it. Thank you very much.

Presenter Well, that's all we've got time for today. Sorry if we didn't have time to take your call, but perhaps you could discuss your questions with your small group leader. Now it's time for the travel news. Over to Cathy Car.

The danger of folly

A short talk
2 mins

Your group members may well wonder what is wrong with being a fool. What's wrong with getting smashed occasionally, or having a good gossip, or being a lazy slob? Well, the book of Proverbs makes it quite clear that foolishness ends in ruin. Explain this to the group and illustrat your point by giving a couple of examples either currently in the news or personally known to you of foolish behaviour that has led to ruin. Two examples spring to mind at the time of writing. First, a 'road rage' attack on a motorway slip road in which one driver lost his temper and stabbed another driver to death. Secondly, a Saturday night incident in our city where a smashed young man attempted to walk along the railing of a bridge and fell thirty feet onto the pavement below. He nearly died and put himself in hospital for a considerable amount of time. These two acts of folly led to long term ruin, and if we persist in foolish behaviour the same could happen to us.

FOOL 001

NAME	Mr Gullible
FAVOURITE OCCUPATION	Swallowing everything whole
MOTTO FOR LIFE	'Take it all on trust.'
WORD OF WARNING	A fool will believe anything; sensible people watch their step. (14:15)

FOOL 002

NAME	Ms Angry
FAVOURITE OCCUPATION	Exploding
MOTTO FOR LIFE	'Blow your top and get i out of your system.'
WORD OF WARNING	People with a hot temper do foolish things; wiser people remain calm. (14:17)

FOOL 003

NAME	Miss Know-it-All
FAVOURITE OCCUPATION	Putting others right
MOTTO FOR LIFE	'Thank God someone knows what they are talking about.'
WORD OF WARNING	Show me a conceited person and I will show you someone who is arrogant, proud and inconsiderate. (21:24)

FOOL 004

NAME	Mr Lazy
FAVOURITE OCCUPATION	Sleeping
MOTTO FOR LIFE	'Oh, I'll just have ten more minutes in bed.'
WORD OF WARNING	Lazy people turn over in bed. They get no further than a door swinging on its hinges. (26:14)

FOOL 005

NAME	Mr Smashed
FAVOURITE OCCUPATION	A quiet drink with the lads.
MOTTO FOR LIFE	'A few beers a day keeps the doctor away.'
WORD OF WARNING	Drinking too much makes you loud and foolish. It is stupid to get drunk. (20:1)

FOOL 006

NAME	Mrs Want-More
FAVOURITE OCCUPATION	Planning her next shopping spree
MOTTO FOR LIFE	'Why settle for less when you can have more?'
WORD OF WARNING	Human desires are like the world of the dead – there is always room for more. (27:20)

FOOL 007

NAME	Master Troublemaker
FAVOURITE OCCUPATION	Planning wicked schemes
MOTTO FOR LIFE	'There's no fun like wicked fun.'
WORD OF WARNING	If you are always planning evil, you will earn a reputation as a troublemaker. (24:8)

FOOL 008

NAME	Mrs Gossip-Liar
FAVOURITE OCCUPATION	Chatting
MOTTO FOR LIFE	'There's nothing like telling a good story.'
WORD OF WARNING	Gossip is spread by wicked people; they stir up trouble & break up friendships.(16:28

MC Solomon song

Sing along with Solomon
2 mins

MC Solomon takes the group through the first few lines of his chant. Play the backing beat and get the group to repeat each line after MC Solomon. Run through the verses so far and finish with the couplet for this week which is as follows.

You will go the foolish way
If you ignore what Proverbs say.

Activities

Party fools

Meet the fools
5 mins

Photocopy the eight fools on page 43, cut them up and give one foolish type to each group member. Explain that you are the host of a party and you want each group member in turn to 'arrive' at your party. When they ring the bell you answer the door and welcome them to the party with a bit of chit chat. *'Hello there! So glad you could come. How are you?',* etc. The party fool has to act throughout in their 'foolish character' so that the other members of the group can guess which fool he or she is as quickly as possible. Once they have correctly guessed fool number one, then enter number two, and so on.

Foolish 'toons

Cartoon strips
10 mins

Divide the group into pairs and ask each pair to pick one of the eight foolish proverbs on page 43 from a hat. Enlarge the 'Foolish 'toons' outline on page 57 by 141% and give each pair a photocopy. Ask them to compose a cartoon strip about a day in the life of their particular fool. If at all possible they should illustrate the kind of ruin that the fool might come to. Once they have had enough time to finish their 'toons, get back together and read them to each other.

60 second fools

A word game
7 mins

Play a game of '60 second fools' in which the contestants have to try to speak for sixty seconds on the subject of one of the eight types of fool without hesitation, deviation or repetition. If the other members of the group think that the speaker has hesitated (um), deviated (gone completely off the point), or repeated any word other than the name of the fool and very little words like 'and', then they can challenge. If you judge the challenge to be correct award the challenger one point and let them take over the subject for the time remaining. If the challenge was not correct then the speaker gains a point and carries on. Remember to stop the clock once a challenge has been made and then start it again when the speaker resumes. Whoever is speaking when the whistle blows at the end of the sixty seconds, gains an extra point. Once you have explained all this ask for a volunteer to start and give them their 'fool' topic. Once the first sixty seconds are up then work your way through some of the other fools, letting a different person start each time. If your group is a bit shy you may have to go first!

Family crests

Design competition
8 mins

Get the group to split into twos or threes and ask each to choose one of the types of fool and design a family crest for that family of fools. If your own family has a family crest then bring it along and explain it to the group. Hand out paper and pens and get them to draw out a shield and ribbon (see illustration) and then get to work. Encourage them to think up a foolish family motto and write it in the ribbon below the crest. If there is time hold a mini exhibition and discuss the crests together.

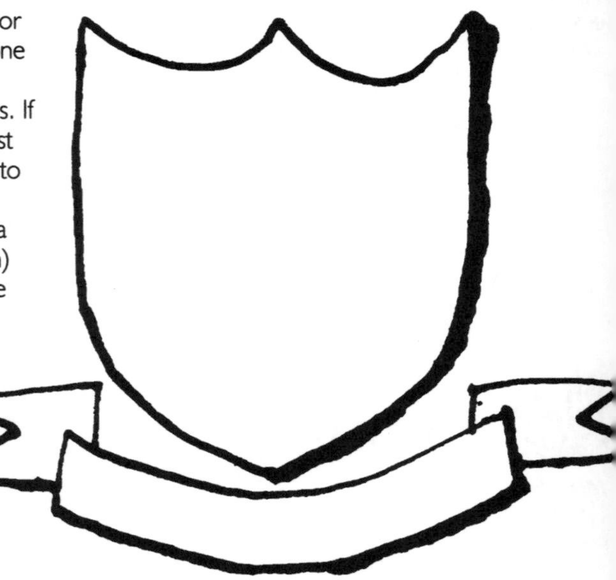

Confessions

Leaders confess all
2 mins

Explain to the group that the reason MC Solomon goes on about fools so much is that he wants to warn us against becoming like them. Go on to confess which fool you feel most in danger of becoming! Then ask the group members which foolish character they are most at r of being. If you are honest with them first, they are more likely to be open with you. Let this lead into the prayer time.

Bottled prayers

Praying together
4 mins

Hand out slips of paper and get the group members to write a prayer asking God to help the not become like the fool they recognise most in themselves. Pass round the prayer bottle so that each person has the opportunity to pray their prayer and bottle it.

Pearls of wisdom

Pondering the proverbs
3 mins

Hand out the shoe laces or copper wires and get the group to thread the third bead (pearl of wisdom). All say the pearl of wisdom together: *'Wisdom is calling out, 'Foolish people! I will give you good advice.'* Then run through the other pearls of wisdom together.

Foolish 'toons

BY

ENLARGE BY 141% (A5–A)

The Acts of the Wise

The Aim: To understand the wisdom of treating others well.

The Lightning Bolt: 'Whenever you possibly can, do good to those who ne it. Never tell your neighbours to wait until tomorrow if you can help them now. Don't plan anything that will hurt your neighbours; they live beside you, trusting yo Proverbs 3:27–29

Equipment Check List

PRESENTATIONS

- ❑ theme music
- ❑ proverb slips & pens
- ❑ 'P on P' tape or video & Wisdometer
- ❑ wisdom bottle and music
- ❑ wisdom clinic sketch props
- ❑ news props & theme tune
- ❑ MC Solomon outfit & music

ACTIVITIES

- ❑ spaghetti letters, plates, card, etc.
- ❑ paper, pens, first line story slips
- ❑ prayer bottle, paper & pens
- ❑ shoe laces & beads
- ❑ copies of daily readings

Letter to leaders

Situations in which we can 'do good to those who need it' range from the blindingly obvious the extremely subtle. I experienced a blindingly obvious situation a few years ago when I hea a man calling out for help as I walked home. At first I couldn't tell where the voice was comir from, but when I looked up I saw a window cleaner stranded on the second floor ledge of a Georgian building. His ladder had been caught by the wind and was lying on the grass. Not t help a chap in such an unfortunate spot would have been unthinkable, and to offer to come back tomorrow would be worse than useless.

Towards the more subtle end of the scale are the situations where we have not been asked help, but where there is clearly a need; perhaps when a colleague is struggling at work, or a neighbour is ill. Then right down the 'extremely-subtle' end are the opportunities that we ca create for being thoughtful towards others; sending a note of thanks to the leaders of your church, or phoning that person who may be feeling lonely. As we get wiser we become mo sensitive to the opportunities for 'doing good' that we can create. And as we take them we become wiser.

- ***Are there any needs, subtle or extreme, that you are aware of at the moment? What can you do to help?***

Help me, my house is on fire !!
Can't you come back tomorrow?

Presentations

Complete the proverb

Write your own ending
4 mins

Play the *Rise Up, Wise Up* theme music as everyone arrives. As they are settling down give group member a pen and slip of paper on which is written the words, 'Whenever you poss can…' Ask each person to complete the proverb in any way they like. Perhaps you could suggest that they take a guess at the theme of the meeting or simply try and produce somet amusing. Once the proverbs have been completed collect them in.

Welcome and introduction

Sparking off
1 min

Give everyone a warm welcome and explain that the subject of the meeting is indeed what you should do *whenever you possibly can*. Read out some of the suggestions that you have collected in and then play the clip of tape in which the *People on the Pavement* attempt to complete the proverb.

The People on the Pavement

Street wise?
2 mins

Play the clip of tape or home-video in which the People on the Pavement complete the phr 'Whenever you possibly can…' Get the group to vote on whether each comment is wise c foolish and reveal their verdict on the Wisdometer.

Message in a bottle

Bottled proverb
2 mins

Play the wisdom bottle music and unveil the bottle. Explain to the group that preliminary X-rays have revealed that the message in the wisdom bottle this week is King Solomon's completion of the proverb, 'Whenever you possibly can...' But unfortunately the rest of the text wasn't clear on the X-ray. So ask for a volunteer to open the bottle, fish out the manuscript and read the completed proverb. The word of wisdom is: *'Whenever you possibly can, do good to those who need it. Never tell your neighbours to wait until tomorrow if you can help them now. Don't plan anything that will hurt your neighbours; they live beside you, trusting you.'*

The wisdom clinic

sketch
4 mins

The scene is a doctor's wisdom clinic, set in a family doctor style consulting room. Set up a desk with a chair either side, angled so that the audience can see both doctor and patient. The sketch consists of a number of patients consulting the doctor about wisdom-related issues.

Cast: DR WISE, MR SMASHED, MRS ANGRY, MISS GOOD.

Dr Wise	*(into his desk microphone)* Would Mr Smashed come through to Room Four, please. *(Mr Smashed staggers in)* Good morning, Mr Smashed, please take a seat. Now what can I do for you?
Mr Smashed	I'se come for my wisdom (hic) check (hic) up.
Dr Wise	Well, before we go any further, may I ask if you have been drinking?
Mr Smashed	Zigackly. I like a glash or two (hic) every now and then.
Dr Wise	Mr Smashed, it is perfectly apparent to me that you are drunk. If you want to become wise you must give up getting smashed. You must limit you alcohol intake to one unit per day. Do I make myself clear?
Mr Smashed	Ferpectly doctor! I'll sgive up straight (hic) away.
Dr Wise	Good. I'll see you again in a fortnight.
Mr Smashed	*(staggering out)* Sank you, doctor. (hic) Did you say there was a pub round the corner? I'll try in there. Scoodbye (hic)
Dr Wise	*(Shakes head, then into microphone)* Would Ms Angry come through to Room Four please. *(Enter Ms Angry who slams door behind her)* Good morning Ms Angry. How are you today?
Ms Angry	DO YOU REALIZE I HAVE BEEN WAITING FOR TWENTY-FIVE MINUTES IN THAT PIT OF A WAITING ROOM. IT'S DISGUSTING! I DON'T PAY GOOD MONEY TO COME HERE AND TWIDDLE MY THUMBS. I HAVE A GOOD MIND TO REPORT YOU TO THE CHIEF INSPECTOR OF WISDOM CLINICS. GOODBYE AND DON'T EXPECT TO SEE ME IN HERE AGAIN!
Dr Wise	*(deep sigh then into desk microphone)* Would Miss Good please come through to Room Four. *(Enter Miss Good)* Good morning, Miss Good. How can I help you?
Miss Good	Good morning doctor. I've come for my monthly wisdom check up.
Dr Wise	OK. Let me just look at your notes from last month... Good... yes... OK. Well, Miss Good, last time I explained the importance of wisdom, and gave you some things to think about. How have you been getting on?
Miss Good	Well, I've thought about what you said and I agree that getting wisdom is the most important thing that I can do in my life, and I understand that the more I learn to respect God the wiser I will become.
Dr Wise	Excellent. That sounds good. OK, if you can just pop your jacket off, I'll listen to your heart. From what you've said it sounds as if it's in the right place, but it's best to be sure. *(Dr Wise listens to Miss Good's heart with a stethoscope or a stethoscope-like object)* Deep breath in... and again... good. You can pop your jacket back on now. Well, Miss Good, I'm pleased to say that your heart is definitely ***in the right***

place which is very important. What you need to do now is keep in good condition. You can do this by exercising your heart regula I'll write you out your wisdom exercise plan here for you. *(He wri on a note pad and as he does so he reads out loud the words he writes.)* 'Whenever you possibly can do good to those who need

Miss Good Er, thank you doctor... er, but I don't think I know any people who need good doing to them.

Dr Wise OK. I'm glad you mentioned that. *(Dr Wise brings out his case boo and points out a few characters who could do with help.)* If you take look here Miss Good I'll show you a few people whom you could possibly help. Firstly there is, er... Lizzie Looking-Lost: that is the n girl at your school. Do you know her?

Miss Good Yes, I do. She's the new girl who is always looking lost.

Dr Wise Well, spending a bit of time with her would be a great exercise. Perhaps just helping her find her way round the school. That is the kind of thing I'm talking about. Then we have, er... Ricardo the Str Kid in Brazil. He could do with some help. Perhaps you could organize a fund-raising event to help him. That's the kind of exerc for your heart that I'm talking about.

Miss Good I see.

Dr Wise And then there is Neil Next-Door-Neighbour: he would apprecia it if you stopped playing loud music late at night. I think that is eno exercise for you to be getting on with. Is that clear or is there any-thing you would like to ask?

Miss Good Well, the thing is, Dr Wise, that I'm rather busy at the moment ar was wondering if it would be OK to put off doing these exercises until tomorrow or just do them once a week?

Dr Wise Well, Miss Good, a lot of people ask that, but the honest answer i no. If you are serious about becoming wise and keeping your hea in good condition it is very important that you do your exercises immediately and regularly. I think I'd better write this on your wisdom exercise plan. *(He writes)* 'Never tell your neighbours to wai until tomorrow if you can help them now.' You see, Miss Good, tomorrow never comes. If you want to get wise you have to do good as often as possible—it is the only way to get your heart in t top condition.

Miss Good OK doctor. I'll do my best. Thank you very much.

Dr Wise *(Miss Good gets up to leave clutching her exercise plan.)* Good bye, Miss Good. Make another appointment for next month. But don't hesitate to come and see me if you need any more advice in the meantime. *(Exit Miss Good.)*

Personal stories

eaders talking 3 mins

Get one or two leaders to briefly tell the group about someone they know and admire for the good they do to others. Give some examples of the kind of good things that this person does and the impact they have on other people's lives. Do include some simple examples of thoughtfulness, and try to conclude by relating it to wisdom.

Here is the news

A news roadcast 2 mins

This item is a news report on the wave of doing good sweeping the country. Play the news theme tune on the audio cassette and read the following script.

Good evening. Here is the news with...(your name). Today the wave of doing good that has been sweeping the country has continued unabated. No old lady has had to cross the road alone since this extraordinary phenomenon began a few weeks ago. Young people have been queuing up by roadside black-spots to help any ancient pedestrians cross the carriageway.

The transformation of 'Neighbourhood Watch' into 'Neighbourhood Act' schemes is symptomatic of this astonishing new trend. No longer do neighbours simply keep an eye out for suspicious characters in the neighbourhood, they now actually act to help each other. They invite each other round for tea, go shopping for each other and have even become good friends.

More astonishingly, a Government report published today revealed that the number of people below the poverty line has dropped dramatically. The explanation for this downward trend is the way the more wealthy members of society are sharing their resources with those in need. The report concludes that if this redistribution of wealth continues at the current rate poverty will be completely wiped out within two years.

And so to the origins of this astonishing wave of doing good. It has become apparent that over the last few months there has been a huge rise in the wisdom rating of our school pupils. Sages from around the world have travelled to this country to witness these remarkable events. The Sagacious Committee on the Propagation of Wisdom have identified the origins of this phenomenon with a desire for practical wisdom among small groups of young people meeting in churches and youth groups all round the country.

That's all we have time for tonight. The next news is at 10 o'clock. Goodnight.

MC Solomon song

ing along h Solomon 2 mins

MC Solomon takes the group through the first four weeks of his song. Play the backing beat and get the group to echo each line he chants. Here is this week's couplet:

If you can help someone today
Do it now—please don't delay.

Activities

Smiles

A game
4 mins

Sit the group in a circle and explain that you are going to throw some smiles around. Start b smiling, then wiping the smile off your face with your hand and throwing it to someone else This person catches it with a smile, shows the smile to everyone then wipes it off and throw to someone else. Keep this going till everyone has had a couple of goes at catching and pass on the smile. The point is that when we do good things to other people it brings a smile int their life.

Spelt out

Spelling the proverb
10 mins

Split the group into teams of three or four. Hand each a tin of spaghetti letters, a tin opener, plate, a sheet of card and a slip of paper on which is written, *'Whenever you possibly can, do good to those who need it.'* Explain that each group is competing against the others to see w will be the first to spell out the verse on the card using the spaghetti letters. It would be a gc idea to have some kitchen towel and a bowl of water ready so they can wash their hands afterwards. (Crosse & Blackwell manufacture 213g tins of Alphabetti Spaghetti letters in Tom Sauce containing more than enough letters.)

On trial

Guilty or not guilty?
10 mins

Paint the scenario that it is now illegal not to help someone who is in any kind of need. Put trial a range of people charged with the criminal offence of *'Withholding help from a person o persons in a state of need'*. Read the charge and then the details of the case (five suggestions below). Then get the group to decide the verdict (guilty or not guilty) and pass sentence as think appropriate (prison, fine, community service, compensation, etc.).

- *On the 16 July Mr Bert Smith was walking home from work when he passed a motorist unable start his/her car. Mr Smith failed to stop as he had an urgent appointment with his television.*
- *Whist on holiday Louise Jones was sunbathing on a quiet beach when she noticed a figure on out at sea waving enthusiastically. She was unsure if this person was in distress or simply wavir friends on the beach and so didn't call the lifeguard. (The waving lilo owner was rescued some hours later by the lifeboat.)*
- *Pete Allan was waiting to catch the bus home from school when he was approached by Larry Liar (an extremely dishonest member of the class). When Larry told Pete that his bus money been stolen and asked if he could borrow some to get home, Pete refused to lend him his spa change.*
- *Jane Bell was with a group of friends at school when the other members of the group started intimidating an unpopular member of the class. Though Jane did not actively take part in the bullying she made no attempt to stop it.*
- *Susie Brown watched a moving and desperate television appeal for money to help famine victi in northern Africa. Having decided to give some money she never actually made the payment*

Good stories

lling tales
10 mins

Split the group into twos or threes, and ask them to devise the plot of a story to follow on from one of the following opening lines. The story must include a good deed by one of the characters. Get back together and tell the stories to each other. Discuss if appropriate.

- *To his horror Golden Delicious realized that he had been picked...*
- *Mrs Octopus looked down at her bicycle tyre in despair. It had a puncture...*
- *'Shiver Me Timbers!' cried desperate pirate captain Smythe...*
- *Grandma Riding Hood was surprised to hear her door bell ring in the middle of the night...*

Wise hearts award

minations
5 mins

Ask each group member to think whom they would like to award a 'Wise Hearts Award' to for their outstanding good deeds. Perhaps it might be a famous charity worker, a friend or relative (Mums win most). Get each person to make their nomination and explain in less than thirty seconds why their candidate deserves the award.

Bottled prayers

Praying together
3 mins

Hand out slips of paper and encourage each group member to write a prayer for someone they know who needs help. Pass round the prayer bottle so that each person can pray their prayer either silently or out loud and then bottle it. Before you pray together make the point that God might want to use members of the group to answer their own prayers. They should bear that in mind when they pray.

Pearls of wisdom

ndering the proverbs
3 mins

Remind the group that the proverbs we are looking at this term are like pearls of wisdom to be treasured. Hand out bead four and ask them to thread it on their shoelace or wire; this represents proverb number four, *'Whenever you possibly can, do good to those who need it.'* Get every one to hold bead four and say the proverb together a couple of times. Then work through the other three beads saying each proverb in turn.

The Loyal Ties of the Wise

The Aim: To understand the wisdom of being loyal.

The Lightning Bolt: 'Never let go of loyalty and faithfulness. Tie them round you neck; write them on your heart. If you do this, both God and people will be pleased with you.' Proverbs 3:3–4

Equipment Check List

PRESENTATIONS

- ❑ theme music
- ❑ 'P on P' tape or video & Wisdometer
- ❑ wisdom bottle & music
- ❑ air-hostess costume, props & tape
- ❑ anatomy OHPs & costume
- ❑ Poet's Corner stool & lamp
- ❑ MC Solomon outfit & music

ACTIVITIES

- ❑ sweets to bribe
- ❑ Mix 'n' Match sheets & pens
- ❑ loyalty self-assessment sheets
- ❑ dog basket or lead
- ❑ prayer bottle, paper & pens
- ❑ shoe laces & beads
- ❑ copies of daily readings

Letter to leaders

I wonder if you have noticed the way children can be a little fickle in their friendships. One week, two of your young people might be as thick as thieves, the next sworn enemies, and before you know it best friends again. Sadly, we don't automatically grow into loyalty as we g[o] older. Even as adults it is much easier to be friends with the people who have something to offer. But fair-weather friendship like that is not loyalty.

Today's proverb makes it clear that loyalty and faithfulness are acts of the will. The sage tells u[s] to **decide** to be loyal to our family, friends and God. It is not a question of being loyal when [we] feel like it. We should tie a commitment of loyalty round our necks and write it in our hearts [so] that whatever the circumstances we act loyally. This makes me think of a stick of rock with th[e] name of a seaside resort running all the way through it. However much you gnaw at the stic[k] or wherever you snap it in half, there in the middle is the word BRIGHTON. Well, the sage wants us to have LOYALTY running through our lives in much the same way.

- ***How loyal are you? Why not take a look at the 'So just how loyal are you?' quiz o[n] page 76 and see how you score. (Adapt the questions accordingly, e.g. change school to work, youth club to church.)***

- ***Have you ever made a conscious decision to be loyal to God, your family and friends? Why not draw up mental list of people you will be loyal to whatever happens?***

CROSS SECTIONS
THROUGH A LOYAL PERSON

Presentations

Welcome and introduction

Sparking off
1 min

Have the *Rise Up, Wise Up* theme music playing as the group arrives and give them all a ver warm welcome. Introduce the session and explain that in today's meeting you will be considering the wisdom of loyalty.

The People on the Pavement

Street wise?
2 mins

Play the clip of tape in which two or three People on the Pavement answer the question, 'W does it mean to be loyal?' After each answer give the group members the chance to vote or the wisdom or folly of each answer and declare the result on the Wisdometer.

Message in a bottle

Bottled proverb
2 mins

Switch on the wisdom bottle theme music and unveil the wisdom bottle. Ask for a voluntee uncork it, fish out the manuscript and read the proverb, which says, *'Never let go of loyalty ar faithfulness. Tie them round your neck; write them on your heart. If you do this, both God and people will be pleased with you.'* Get the group to say the proverb together a few times.

Safety instructions

Air hostess sketch
3 mins

This is a very simple sketch based on the bizarre way air hostesses explain the safety instructions on aeroplane flights. An air hostess (suitably dressed up) stands at the front of the plane (room) and for the *n*th time mimes illustrations to the instructions that are being read c over the tannoy (read by a leader at the back of the room holding her nose). The air hostes needs to have her actions well planned and rehearsed. There are some suggestions in the margin on the right of the following script. You can easily make a 'loyalty' life jacket from sor card and string, and cut the heart out of red paper or card.

BING BONG! Ladies and gentlemen, good morning and welcome to Wisdom Airways flight L-I-F-E. Your pilot today is MC Solomon and your hostesses Faith and Prudence. We hope you will enjoy your journey. As you know we are travelling at sixty minutes per hour, twenty four hours per day towards our final encounter with God. Our time of arrival in heaven is unknown, but our flight will take you all the way there, so wise up and enjoy the journey.

Hostess stands at front smiling

Your Hostess Prudence will now demonstrate some of the features of the aeroplane for your interest and safety on the journey. There are folly exits for anyone foolish enough to want to disembark from the plane in mid-

flight. These are situated at the rear of the plane on the right and left.[1] We strongly advise you not[2] to use them and warn you that if you do you will encounter God before your correct time of arrival.

1. signal doors at back on right & left
2. shake head and cross arms in sweeping movement

In the rack in front of you[3] you will find a booklet of wisdom proverbs and a plan of the aeroplane. In the consul above your head[4] you have wisdom lights to light your journey, and a 'sage call' button should you wish to have any personal wisdom tuition.

3. display Bible
4. indicate consul above head

Lastly, a few safety instructions for the flight. If you look under your seat you will find that you have been issued with some loyalty and faithfulness.[5] These have been provided to make your journey more satisfying so please use them wisely like this:[6] hold on tight to your loyalty and faithfulness in all situations.[7] Tie them round your neck so that they are always there when you need them.[8] Write them on your heart so that you use them instinctively. If you do this both God[9] and your fellow passengers[10] on Wisdom Airways flight L-I-F-E will be pleased with you.

5. display loyalty & faithfulness life jacket
6. hold jacket tight
7. loop ties round head then remove
8. produce heart and write on it
9. point up
10. arms open towards group

Ladies and gentlemen, thank you for being wise enough to travel with Wisdom Airways. Please rise up, wise up and enjoy the flight.[11] Thank you. BING BONG.

11. big smile

An anatomy of loyalty

A lecture
3 mins

A professor of anatomy gives a short illustrated lecture on the anatomy of a loyal person. Photocopy the pictures on pages 70 & 71 onto two acetates. Cut up the second acetate along the dotted lines and tape the edges to the sides of the first so the speech bubbles can be easily laid over the first picture in the correct positions. The proportions of the different anatomical features have been adjusted to show their relative importance in the anatomy of a loyal person. Dress up one of the leaders as a professor of anatomy (lab coat and wig) and get him/her to talk the group through the seven key anatomical features of the loyal person. For each one s/he folds over the appropriate speech bubble giving an example of how the feature might be used. These are as follows:

- **heart that cares...** *'You poor thing!'*
- **lips that tell you the truth...** *'No, I don't think you should go out with him.'*
- **ears that listen...** *'Yes, I hear what you're saying.'*
- **solid shoulder to lean on...** *'Feel free to lean on me in a crisis.'*
- **hands ready to help...** *'Do let me help dig your car out of that lorry load of manure.'*
- **feet that are there when you need them...** *'Don't worry. We're coming right round.'*
- **generally very sticky all over...** *'I'll stick by you whatever happens.'*

YES I HEAR WHAT YOU'RE SAYING
FEEL FREE TO LEAN ON ME IN A CRISIS
NO, I REALLY DON'T THINK YOU SHOULD GO OUT WITH HIM!
YOU POOR THING!
WE'LL HELP YOU DIG YOUR CAR OUT OF THAT LORRY LOAD OF MANURE
I'LL STICK BY YOU WHATEVER HAPPENS.
DONT WORRY WE'RE COMING RIGHT ROUND

Poet's Corner
2 mins

Best friends

Set up a stool in a corner of the room, dim the lights, point an angle-poise lamp at the stool and introduce this weeks guest on Poet's Corner. Dress up one of the leaders (male or fema as the archetypal school girl, get them to sit on the stool and read the following poem by Adrian Henri.

Best Friends

It's Susan I talk to not Tracey,
Before that I sat next to Jane;
I used to be best friends with Lynda
But these days I think she's a pain.

Natasha's all right in small doses,
I meet Mandy sometimes in town;
I'm jealous of Annabel's pony
And I don't like Nicola's frown.

I used to go skating with Catherine,
Before that I went there with Ruth;
And Kate's so much better at trampoline:
She's a showoff to tell you the truth.

I think that I'm going off Susan,
She borrowed my comb yesterday;
I *think* I might sit next to Tracey,
She's my nearly best friend: she's OK.

Adrian Henri

Leader speaks out
2 mins

Heart to heart

Tell the group about a loyal friend, relative or pet of yours and the difference they have made your life. Try and give practical illustrations of ways they have been loyal to you and how that has affected you. Keep it short and sweet, and certainly no longer than two minutes.

Sing along with Solomon
2 mins

MC Solomon song

MC Solomon takes the group through the first five weeks of his song. Play the backing beat a get the group to repeat each line after MC Solomon. Here is this week's couplet:

Here is how to be a good friend
Be loyal and faithful to the end.

Activities

The price of loyalty

attempted bribe
4 mins

Get each group member to write down on a separate slip of paper someone or something of which they are a fan (e.g. football club or pop star). Then bring out a bag of sweets and explain that you will give three sweets to anyone who stands up and denounces as being 'rubbish' the thing or person written on their slip of paper. If no one will do the dastardly deed then increase the reward till you get someone to take the bait. If no one is prepared to be disloyal for mere sweets then that makes the point just as well.

Mix 'n' match

Pairing Proverbs
4 mins

Below is a list of ten loyalty proverbs split in two. The idea of this activity is for the group members to try and correctly match the first and second half of each proverb. Write out the second halves of the ten proverbs below on separate sheets of paper and stick them round the walls of your meeting room. Give each member of the group a photocopy of the worksheet listing the first halves of the proverbs (on page 74). Hand out pens and get them to go round the room and try to match the first and second halves of the proverbs. When they have finished, run through the correct answers so they can see how they got on.

- *Depending on an unreliable person in a crisis ... is like trying to chew with a loose tooth. 25:19*
- *Remembering wrongs can ... break up a friendship. 17:9*
- *Loyalty is what is desired in a person ... poor people are better off than liars. 19:22*
- *Friends always show their love ... What are relatives for if not to share trouble? 17:17*
- *An honest answer is a ... sign of true friendship. 24:26*
- *Never let go of loyalty and faithfulness ... If you do this, both God and people will be pleased with you. 3:3,4*
- *Some friendships do not last but ... some friends are more loyal than brothers. 18:24*
- *People learn from one another ... just as iron sharpens iron. 27:17*
- *Be loyal and faithful, and ... God will forgive your sin. 16:6*
- *Everyone talks about how loyal and faithful he is ... but just try to find someone who really is! 20:6*

Lightning sketches

xploring the proverbs
10 mins

Split into smaller groups and give each group one of the loyalty proverbs used in the Mix 'n' Match activity and ask them to produce a lightning sketch exploring what it means. For example, a sketch based on the proverb, *'An honest answer is a sign of true friendship.'* might involve two girls getting dressed up for a party. One of them puts on a very weird outfit (improvised from whatever is available) and wants to know what her friend thinks. The sketch could explore the range of possible answers and their consequences. Once everyone has produced their sketch, get back together and perform them to each other. Hand each group three random props, and they will find preparing the sketch much more interesting.

Loyalty Proverbs

Find the second half of each of these 'loyalty proverbs'.

Depending on an unreliable person in a crisis . . . .

Remembering wrongs can . . . .

Loyalty is what is desired in a person . . . .

Friends always show their love . . . .

An honest answer is a . . . .

Never let go of loyalty and faithfulness . . . .

Some friendships do not last but . . . .

People learn from one another . . . .

Be loyal and faithful, and . . . .

Everyone talks about how loyal and faithful he is . . . .

Loyalty Proverbs

Find the second half of each of these 'loyalty proverbs'.

Depending on an unreliable person in a crisis . . . .

Remembering wrongs can . . . .

Loyalty is what is desired in a person . . . .

Friends always show their love . . . .

An honest answer is a . . . .

Never let go of loyalty and faithfulness . . . .

Some friendships do not last but . . . .

People learn from one another . . . .

Be loyal and faithful, and . . . .

Everyone talks about how loyal and faithful he is . . . .

So how loyal are you?

A self-assessment quiz
7 mins

Hand each member of the group a copy of the 'So just how loyal are you?' self-assessment quiz on page 76 and give them about five minutes to complete it. Then explain how the scores work. For questions 1, 2, 4, 7, 10 score two points for each 'yes' answer and 0 points for each 'no' answer. For questions 3, 5, 6, 8 and 9 score 2 points for each 'no' answer and 0 points for each 'yes'. For all 'not sures' score 1 point. The nearer the scores are to twenty the more loyal you are. If you feel it is appropriate perhaps they could discuss how they've done or some of the individual questions.

Dog loyal

Brain-storming
4 mins

Dogs are the archetypal loyal creature; loyal to their owners no matter what happens. A classic example of this is the case of Charles Gough a gentleman sketcher who in 1805 fell from Striding Edge whilst climbing Helvellyn in the English Lake District. Three months later his dog, an Irish terrier, was found faithfully guarding his remains. (William Wordsworth and Walter Scott both wrote poems describing the tragedy and emphasising the heroic and faithful dog.) The aim of the following activity is to find out what we can learn about loyalty from dogs.

Get hold of a dog's lead, collar or basket. Tell the story of Charles Gough to the group and then ask them to try and brainstorm for other examples of dog loyalty (e.g. waiting by the front door for you to come home, guarding the home, coming when called, etc.) Try and get as many ideas as there are group members. Write all these on separate slips of paper and place them in the dog's basket or pin them to the lead. Then get each group member to pick a slip and think of an example of how we can be loyal in a similar way (either to God or our family and friends). Perhaps you could also discuss what it means to tie loyalty round your neck and write it on your heart.

Bottled prayers

Praying together
4 mins

Ask each group member to make a list of people they will be loyal to from now on. Then encourage them to write a prayer asking God to help them be dog loyal. Pass the prayer bottle so that everyone can pray silently and bottle their prayer.

Pearls of wisdom

The proverb
2 mins

Hand out the shoe laces or wire and get the group to thread the fifth bead (pearl of wisdom). All say the pearl of wisdom together: *'Never let go of loyalty and faithfulness.'* Then run through the other pearls of wisdom together.

So just how loyal are you?

Answer the following questions and find out how you fare on the loyalty stakes.

	yes	not sure	no
1. A friend helps you enter a magazine competition and you win £50. Would you share the dosh?	❑	❑	❑
2. You overhear some people in your class slagging off your friend. Would you interrupt to defend him or her?	❑	❑	❑
3. A friend seems to be rather depressed and is not much fun to be with any more. Would you back off till they were back to normal again?	❑	❑	❑
4. You are off to a party with a friend. They're wearing a new outfit which looks truly 'sad'. They ask you what you think. Would you tell the truth?	❑	❑	❑
5. One of your friends at school suddenly becomes very unpopular for no good reason. Would you become less friendly too?	❑	❑	❑
6. A friend asks you to hide some fags for them for a few days. Would you do it?	❑	❑	❑
7. You have accepted an invitation to a friend's party. Later in the week you get an invitation to the party of that boy/girl you really fancy which is on the same night. Would you go to the first party?	❑	❑	❑
8. Some kids in your class at school start telling everyone that the church youth group you go to is rubbish. Would you keep your head down and stay out of it?	❑	❑	❑
9. A friend has lent you £5 and seems to have forgotten about it. Would you also 'forget' to repay it?	❑	❑	❑
10. A friend's Mum phones just as you are about to settle down in front of the TV and watch your fav show. Her son/daughter is fed up and would really like you to come over. Would you go?	❑	❑	❑

So just how loyal are you?

Answer the following questions and find out how you fare on the loyalty stakes.

	yes	not sure	no
1. A friend helps you enter a magazine competition and you win £50. Would you share the dosh?	❑	❑	❑
2. You overhear some people in your class slagging off your friend. Would you interrupt to defend him or her?	❑	❑	❑
3. A friend seems to be rather depressed and is not much fun to be with any more. Would you back off till they were back to normal again?	❑	❑	❑
4. You are off to a party with a friend. They're wearing a new outfit which looks truly 'sad'. They ask you what you think. Would you tell the truth?	❑	❑	❑
5. One of your friends at school suddenly becomes very unpopular for no good reason. Would you become less friendly too?	❑	❑	❑
6. A friend asks you to hide some fags for them for a few days. Would you do it?	❑	❑	❑
7. You have accepted an invitation to a friend's party. Later in the week you get an invitation to the party of that boy/girl you really fancy which is on the same night. Would you go to the first party?	❑	❑	❑
8. Some kids in your class at school start telling everyone that the church youth group you go to is rubbish. Would you keep your head down and stay out of it?	❑	❑	❑
9. A friend has lent you £5 and seems to have forgotten about it. Would you also 'forget' to repay it?	❑	❑	❑
10. A friend's Mum phones just as you are about to settle down in front of the TV and watch your fav show. Her son/daughter is fed up and would really like you to come over. Would you go?	❑	❑	❑

Thoughts of Wisdom

The Aim: To inspire everyone to watch the way they think.

The Lightning Bolt: 'Be careful how you think; your life is shaped by your thoughts.' Proverbs 4:23

Equipment Check List

PRESENTATIONS

- ❑ theme music
- ❑ 'P on P' tape or video & Wisdometer
- ❑ Wisdom bottle and music
- ❑ botany for beginners props
- ❑ post mortem sketch kit
- ❑ Shape-up Shirley music & kit
- ❑ MC Solomon outfit & music

ACTIVITIES

- ❑ plasticine & thought slips
- ❑ large thought bubbles
- ❑ prayer bottle, paper & pens
- ❑ shoe laces & beads
- ❑ copies of daily readings

Letter to leaders

Being careful how you think is certainly easier said than done. I have a friend whose life has been somewhat hijacked by his overactive romantic imagination. He is obsessed with a girl, who is not the slightest bit interested. His thoughts seize on any crumb of hope and turn it into a banquet of possibilities. His life is most certainly being shaped (seriously constricted) by his thoughts.

But how do we control our thoughts? My experience is that they seem to have a life of their own. They always come back to, and embellish on, the things you wish you'd never seen, never heard of, or never done. Is it even possible to control them? Well, here are two suggestions, neither of which are instant cures to wayward thinking. The first is to minimise your intake of 'unhelpful' images, words and experiences. Wherever possible avoid seeing or experiencing the unhelpful things that your mind has a tendency to dwell on. Be careful which films you watch and which magazines you read. Secondly, when your thoughts are heading down one of those smelly alleyways, break the chain and fill your mind with something else - read a good book, phone a friend, seize control. I know it's a battle, but if we want to be wise we must do all we can to control our thoughts because they will shape our life one way or the other.

- ***Are there any particular thought patterns that you need to guard against?***
- ***Why not talk to God about how you can best seize control and then ask him to give you the will power to do it?***

Presentations

Welcome and introduction

Sparking off
1 min

Play the *Rise Up, Wise Up* theme music as the group arrives. Give everyone a warm welcom and explain that in this week's *Rise Up, Wise Up* meeting you will be delving into the murky world of the mind. You will be examining what King Solomon has to say about the way we think and the way our thoughts affect our behaviour.

The People on the Pavement

Street wise?
2 mins

Play the tape clip in which the *People on the Pavement* answer the question, 'What do you thi most affects the way a person behaves?' Get the group to vote on whether each comment is wise or foolish and reveal their verdict on the Wisdometer.

Message in a bottle

Bottled proverb
2 mins

Switch on the wisdom bottle theme music and unveil the bottle itself. Ask for a volunteer to open the bottle, fish out the manuscript and read the ancient words of wisdom from King Solomon. The words of wisdom that should be written on the scrap of age-old parchment a as follows: *'Be careful how you think; your life is shaped by your thoughts.'*

Botany for beginners

A horticultural illustration
3 mins

This is a simple demonstration making the point that ***what you plant is what you get***. A botanist (dressed in lab coat, etc.) starts by demonstrating some simple principles of botany. S/he takes a pot of soil and a pack of seeds and explains that if, for example, you plant primro seeds (s/he demonstrates) a few months later you get primroses ('Here are some I prepared earlier'). If you plant daffodil bulbs you get daffodils because 'what you plant is what you get'. S/he then goes on to apply this fundamental principle of horticulture to planting thoughts as follows:

- *If you plant greedy thoughts you get greedy actions.*
- *If you plant selfish thoughts you get selfish actions.*
- *If you plant hateful thoughts you get hateful actions.*
- *If you plant generous thoughts you get generous actions.*
- *If you plant kind thoughts you get kind actions.*

A nasty case of thought abuse

A post mortem sketch
3 mins

This post mortem investigation sketch makes the point that what goes on in our head shapes our life and ultimately our death. The scene is a mortuary. A body lies on a table covered in a white sheet. A tag hangs from its big toe. A professor of pathology and a pathology student (both in white coats) enter and set out to discover the cause of the deceased's death. Here is a rough script for you to work round.

Cast: PROFESSOR, STUDENT and BODY.

	Enter Professor and Student
Prof.	...That was the thirteenth case of fatal 'thought-abuse' I've seen this week, and it's only Tuesday.
Student	Is that much more than normal, Professor?
Prof.	Oh no. It's always the most common cause of expiration in humans. From what I've been told our next customer is a particularly severe case. Ahhh, here we are, No 5682. *(They lift the sheet in such a way that the group can't see what is beneath it.)* You hold that there while I take a look at this poor blighter.
Student	*(sharp intake of breath.)* Oh dear, that is a bad one! What do you think it is?
Prof.	Well, for a start we've got an obvious case of 'hardened-heart'.
Student	What causes that?
Prof.	Oh, it's invariably the result of compounded selfish thinking. But to get a heart that is this badly hardened, he must have been a chain selfish thinker from childhood. *(pause)* Mmmm, it looks as if he's also got a particularly unpleasant case of blood poisoning. You see the blood has a slightly greenish tinge. That is always caused by sustained jealous thinking.
Student	Is that why they say 'Jealous thoughts are poisonous thoughts'?
Prof.	Yes, indeed. *(pause)* Just as I thought, if you look at his eyes you'll see that he's also got bad 'eye-rot'.
Student	What causes that Prof.?
Prof.	Well, it could be a number of things, all of which involve sustained looking at degrading, violent and immoral images and then dwelling on them in your mind. Video nasties, obscene magazines, that kind of thing.
Student	Would that mean that he is likely to have 'brain-rot' as well?
Prof.	That is exactly right. Well done, you've obviously been studying hard. Eye-rot is often linked to brain-rot, otherwise known as 'rotting-brain', though it is of course not the only cause of brain-rot. It is associated with a number of dangerous thought patterns: proud thoughts, bitter thoughts, angry thoughts and of course cruel thoughts.
Student	Prof., what do you make of his hands and arms? They are incredibly swollen and puffy. I've never seen anything like it.
Prof.	Ahh. That's a classic case of 'grabbit-arm'. You see, what happens is this: the brain sends out a lot of greedy thoughts, 'Want this, want that!' and so the arms are always grabbing things and clutching onto them. And of course they get damaged in the process. Rather like being burnt.
Student	Poor chap!
Prof.	Well, not really! I mean he brought, or thought, it on himself! *(pause)* Ah, now he's also got an interesting case of 'black-lung'. That is caused by spend-

ing a lot of time in bad atmosphere, in bad company. And of course as w as affecting the lungs this will have been part of the cause of the brain-rot.

Student Is that it?

Prof. Yes, I think that's all we can say about this gentleman. So could you write the records, 'Cause of Death: Chronic Thought-Abuse leading to Severe Hardened-Heart, Blood-Poisoning, Eye and Brain-Rot, Grabbit-Arm and advanced Black Lung.'

Student If the general public could see what 'thought-abuse' can do to your life th they would jolly well control their thoughts a bit more carefully.

Prof. Yes indeed. *(pause)* Well, I think it's time for coffee.

Mind-robics
4 mins

Shape-up Shirley

Just as we need to keep our bodies in trim with physical work-outs so we need to give our minds a regular mental work-out. Lycra-clad Shape-up Shirley takes the group through a physical and mental work-out. Here are some suggestions:

Play some aerobic-style music and take the group through some aerobic exercises (stretch, two, three, four, five, six, seven, eight, etc.) Consult an aerobics enthusiast for some suitable exercises and music.

Turn off the music and go on to do some mental exercises. Get everyone sitting cross-legge on the floor, with their hands in their laps and close their eyes. Then lead them through the following mental aerobics exercises.

- *Count from one to twenty in your head. (Excellent - well done!)*
- *Now think of your favourite song. Run through the words and tune in your mind. (Good!)*
- *Now imagine you are walking alone along a beach as the sun sets over the sea... Feel the sea breeze on your face, smell the salt air... Listen to the waves breaking on the shore... Sense the sand under your feet... (Fantastic!)*
- *Now picture a corridor in your mind... Walk down it... There are doors on either side of the corridor... Choose a door that represents the part of your mind where your mum is... Knock ar enter... Think what you would like to say to her... Why not give her a hug?*
- *Now knock at the door of the room that represents someone who really annoys you... Go in ar think of one good thing about this person... Say it to them now in your mind... (Good!)*
- *Now come back into the corridor and walk to the end and out into the daylight where you see something very beautiful... Look at it and admire it... (Great!) Now open your eyes and look around you and relax.*

Shape-up Shirley concludes the work-out saying something like, *'Well done, good work-out! V that's it for today, but remember that for a healthy body you need healthy thoughts. Working to keep your thoughts in trim is vital to a wise and healthy life. Take a shower.'*

HAPPY BIRTH

MC Solomon song

Sing along with Solomon
2 mins

MC Solomon takes the group through the first six weeks of his song. Play the backing beat a get the group to repeat each line after MC Solomon. Here is this week's couplet:

Watch what goes on in your head:
By your thoughts your life is led.

Activities

Shape it

Plasticine charades
5 mins

Remind the group of the word of wisdom for the day, *'Be careful how you think; your life is shaped by your thoughts.'* Explain that the way you think shapes the way you behave. Perhap you could get the group to recap on the point of the botanist sketch. Then give each group member a slip of paper on which is written one of the kind of thoughts listed below. Hand someone a lump of plasticine and explain that it represents a person's life. Ask them to demonstrate (mime) how the thought written on their slip of paper might shape the life (the plasticine). For example, if the thought was 'violent' they might shape the plasticine with very violent actions, if it was 'gentle' they might shape it very tenderly. (What matters is not the shape you make the plasticine into but the actions and manner with which you shape it.) Th others have to guess what the original thought was. Let everyone have a go at shaping the plasticine with their 'thought'.

- *violent*
- *loving*
- *excited*
- *cruel*
- *sad*
- *proud*
- *gentle*
- *happy*
- *romantic*
- *nervous*

Be careful how you think...

Proverb on board
6 mins

Sit the group in a circle and say the proverb together a few times. Then turn it into a game. Explain that you will say the proverb personally to a group member (John), *'Be careful how y think* **John***; your life is shaped by your thoughts.'* The idea is that you try and make John smile the manner or feeling with which you say the words. He however must take it seriously (without smiling) and then say it to someone else personally and try and make them smile by the way he says it. Once a group member succumbs to the irrepressible urge to smile they 'out'. Carry on like this for about five minutes. Some clues to forcing a smile out of the group members include: funny accents, strange word emphasis, dramatic gestures and eccentric mannerisms.

ightning ketches
10 mins

Thought bubbles

Split into groups of about three or four and hand each a large thought bubble (cardboard cut out) with one of the following thoughts written in it. Ask them to produce a little sketch illustrating where that thought might lead. Then get back together and perform them to each other and discuss if appropriate. Here are some sample thoughts to write in the bubbles:

- *'Phwoarr! He's a bit of all right.'*
- *'I love my mum.'*
- *'That girl's trainers are just soooo sad!'*
- *'What a beautiful day! Doesn't it make you feel good to be alive!'*
- *'I'm flipping furious with Johnny. Boy, is he going to regret doing that!'*
- *'I wish I had parents like that.'*

debate
10 mins

Does it really?

Debate or discuss the following motion, *'The way you think affects the way you behave.'* Split into two teams and give each five minutes to prepare the argument and evidence for or against the motion. Encourage them to think up concrete examples of how it does or doesn't affect the way you behave, e.g. Does watching violence on TV affect your behaviour? Does watching sport make you want to play sport? Then get back together and debate it properly or simply discuss. Perhaps you could take a vote at the end.

If this develops naturally into a discussion it might be appropriate to give the group some advice on how to deal with troublesome thoughts or recurring mental imagery. Here are some possibly helpful tips:

- *Try to avoid those films, books, people, etc. who feed you with thoughts that you find disturbing.*
- *Ask God to take away those thoughts and forgive you for having them.*
- *Actively try and fill your mind with good thoughts (read the right sort of book, or watch the right sort of TV programme).*

Praying together
3 mins

Bottled wisdom

Hand everyone a piece of 'thought bubble' shaped paper and a pen and encourage them to write a prayer asking God to help them learn to control their thoughts. Perhaps they could be more specific and pray about particular thoughts that trouble them. When they are ready, pass round the prayer bottle so that everyone can pray their prayer out loud or silently and then bottle it.

ndering the proverbs
3 mins

Pearls of wisdom

Hand out the shoe laces or wires and get the group to thread the sixth bead (pearl of wisdom). All say the pearl of wisdom together: *'Be careful how you think; your life is shaped by your thoughts.'* Then run through the other pearls of wisdom together.

At Home with Wisdom

The Aim: To understand why it's wise to respect those who are bringing us up

The Lightning Bolt: 'Wise children make their fathers proud of them; foolis
ones bring their mothers grief.' Proverbs 10:1

Equipment Check List

PRESENTATIONS
- ❑ theme music
- ❑ photos of leaders & parents, paper & pens
- ❑ 'P on P' tape or video & Wisdometer
- ❑ wisdom bottle and music
- ❑ sound effects for Parent Watch
- ❑ tape or video of parent's answers
- ❑ Poet's Corner stool & lamp
- ❑ MC Solomon outfit & music

ACTIVITIES
- ❑ role play slips
- ❑ paper & pens
- ❑ prayer bottle, paper & pens
- ❑ shoe laces & beads
- ❑ copies of daily readings

Letter to leaders

Talking 'family' can be a bit tricky. Many young people these days are having a tough time at home and feel betrayed or let down by their parents. (Perhaps it has always been like that - just more out in the open now.) The sage, however, agrees with the Fifth Commandment a says that children should honour their parents. He doesn't say anything about parents that d deserve to be honoured, or parents who abuse their children.

Maybe there is a sound principle here. In the end we are only accountable to God for the w **we** behave. We are not accountable to God for the behaviour of our parents. However go or bad our parents may have been, God still wants us to live good and wise lives ourselves. understands that this will be tough if our parents have put us through hell, but he wants us t do what we can to live in peace with others.

This may not be what some of the children in your group need to hear at this moment of t lives. Those who are suffering at home will just need to know that you care and will listen. Others, however, will need to know that it is very foolish to be a pain in the neck at home, yet others will need encouragement to keep trying to be wise.

- ***Think about your group members. Do you feel that any of them could do with a of understanding and support from you concerning their home situation?***
- ***Why not pray for each member of your group now?***

resentations

Leaders have parents too

ix and Match
5 mins

This is a game in which the group members have to try and match photos of the youth group leaders with photos of their parents. Each leader needs to bring 2 photos to the meeting: one of themselves, and one of their parents. (If you only have a few leaders in the team try and get hold of photos of church leaders and their parents.) Stick each photo onto a separate card. Label the leader photos A, B, C, etc. and pin them around the room. Label the parent photos 1, 2, 3, etc. and pin them up too. When the group arrives hand out slips of paper and pens and ask them to go round the room and try and match up the leaders with their parents. (Play the *Rise Up, Wise Up* theme music as they do this.) After about five minutes get everyone together and run through the correct answers. Go on to explain that in this week's *Rise Up, Wise Up* meeting you will be exploring what King Solomon has to say about wisdom in the home, and most particularly in relation to the people who bring us up.

The People on the Pavement

eet wise?
2 mins

Play the clip of tape or the home-video in which the People on the Pavement answer the question, '*How should children treat those who are bringing them up?*' Get the group to vote on the wisdom or folly of each answer and declare the verdict on the Wisdometer.

Message in a bottle

ottled proverb
2 mins

Produce the wisdom bottle containing the words '*Wise children make their fathers proud of them; foolish ones bring their mothers grief.*' Play the wisdom bottle music and ask for a volunteer to open the bottle, fish out the manuscript and read the proverb.

A parent tells all

illing the beans
4 mins

Arrange for the parent(s) of one of the leaders to tell the group about their experiences bringing up their son or daughter. Do encourage them to include some amusing anecdotes from the leader's childhood and let the group members ask questions too. They will love this. If you run this feature as an interview, here are some questions you could use:

- *What was X like as a child?*
- *How did s/he get on with her/his brothers or sisters?*
- *Do any funny incidents stick in your mind?*
- *Could you give us an example of something they did that really upset you?*
- *How did this make you feel?*
- *Was there any time when you knew they were doing something that was not good for them? What did you do?*
- *What fears did you have for them as they were growing up?*
- *What did you hope for them? Did they fulfil your hopes?*

MUM! DAD!
Can I go for a bike ride now?
Well, I hope you're proud of him!

Parent watch

cumentary
4 mins

This feature is a nature documentary investigating the incredible relationship between human parents and their offspring. It should be done in a rather detached way, almost as if an alien is observing some incomprehensible phenomenon. Here is a rough script for you to work round. Read the script as if it were a radio broadcast and play the sound effects on the audio cassette in the appropriate places.

PARENT WATCH THEME TUNE
Narrator: *(in a breathless and hushed voice)* Hello, and welcome to 'Parent Watch'. In today's programme we will be investigating the extraordinary relationship between parent and offspring in the species Homo Sapiens—otherwise known as human beings. Though the gestation period of the female is not the longest of all mammals (being only 9 months), the care and rearing of her offspring can last over sixty years. We have secretly set up our cameras in three different human family groups and we are going to take a look at what is going on in each. Our first camera is hidden in the home of one female who has recently given birth to a baby boy whom she has named Ernest.
BABY SCREAMING ITS HEAD OFF SOUND EFFECTS
This is astonishing! There she is, holding the baby, who is making the most appalling noise for no apparent reason. It is fascinating how human babies can make a noise that is so disproportionate to their size. This screaming can go on for up to twenty-three hours a day.
MORE BABY SCREAMING
Up to the birth, the mother had spent her time doing her own thing: meeting friends, working, and enjoying herself, and then suddenly with the birth of her baby she is happy to throw it all up to look after this wrinkly little windbag.

We are now going to turn the clock forward a few months. Here you see the baby has stopped crying and has learnt to smile. Note the effect one smile has on the parents! They reply by returning the smile and making strange gooey noises. These parents, however, still have their hands quite full.
SICKY NOISE
Did you hear that?! The baby has just vomited over his new romper suit and managed to get it all over the settee too. Watch how the mother patiently clears it up, changes the babies' clothes and washes down the sofa. Amazing.
NAPPY SOUND EFFECTS
Oh dear! Now the baby's nappy needs changing too...

We are now going to take a look at the pictures our second camera is bringing us. This camera is hidden in the kitchen of another human family. The three offspring of this couple are aged eight, six and three years. Here we see them seated round the table for a communal meal. The father has just spent the last two hours slaving over the stove producing what we believe is a chick pea lasagne. He now careful shares out the portions and places them on the table in front of each of his offspring. How do they respond? Well, the eight year-old has refused to touch it, the six year-old has eaten a couple of mouthfuls and, oh this is extraordinary, the three year-old has thrown his portion on the floor.
CLATTERING PLATE AND SPLAT SOUND EFFECTS
The father, visibly strained, is now clearing it up.

Let's now switch to our third and final camera which is positioned in a street sign outside number 52 North Road in (your town). Here we see a human father sitting in a car waiting. is waiting to collect his son from a noisy gathering of the human species, otherwise known as party.

MUFFLED PARTY SOUND EFFECTS

He has been sitting there for forty five minutes. He arranged to collect his son at 10 p.m. but 10.15 his son came out to say he had to stay for another fifteen minutes. That was half an hc ago. Oh, here comes the son, he gets into the car and the father drives off patiently.

CAR DOOR SLAMMING AND CAR DRIVING OFF SOUND EFFECTS

So, we've seen how this relationship between parents and their offspring develops from putti up with screaming, sick and nappies, through to ungrateful behaviour and irresponsible thoughtlessness. Who'd be a human parent! But despite all this the parents still love and care for their offspring in the most astonishing way. Well, that's all we've got time for this week. N week we will be looking at the way koalas bring up their offspring. Good bye.

PARENT WATCH THEME TUNE

What would your parents do?

Children on parents quiz
4 mins

To run this feature to maximum effect you need to do a little extra work the week before. Th idea is that in the meeting you invite a couple of group members up the front and ask them what their parents would do in the situations listed below. Unbeknown to them you have previously contacted their parents and asked them what they would do in these same situations. If possible tape or video their answers. Once you have interviewed the two group members explain that you have asked their parents these same questions and then play the tape. This has a very dramatic effect and stimulates a great deal of group discussion, the aim c which is to help the group see their parent's side of the story. Make sure you choose young people who could cope with the shock.

- *What would your parents do if they thought you had been smoking?*
- *What would your parents say if you asked if you could have your ears pierced?*
- *What would your parents do if you came home one day with your hair bleached?*
- *What would you parents say if you asked if you could have a party at home?*
- *What would your parents do if you got a really bad school report?*
- *What would your parents do if your new boy/girl friend was not really their type?*

Poet's Corner

A poem
2 mins

Set up the Poet's Corner stool and spotlight. Then introduce the poet of the week and get them to read the poem, 'Parents Can Be Hard Work' printed out below.

Parents Can Be Hard Work

Parents can be hard work
They can be a pain
But even when they hassle you
Don't flush them down the drain

Your dad may try and tell you
Just who your friends should be
But even if this is a cheek
Don't send him off to sea.

Your mum may change your diet
Say you're too fat or thin
But even if this bugs you
Don't chuck her in the bin

Your Pa may ask you questions
On what you do all day
But even if he's nosy
Don't hold back all his pay

Your Ma may not have grasped
The generation gap
But even if she's out of touch
Don't sell her off for scrap

Your father may complain
About the way you speak
But even if this winds you up
Don't ground him for a week

Your mother may embarrass you
She may make you cringe
But next time she's being naff
Don't load up your syringe

Though parents can be hard
Smart children realize
Our old folks are God's gift to us
To help us to be wise

MC Solomon Song

g along with Solomon *2 mins*

MC Solomon takes the group through the first six weeks of his song. Play the backing beat and get the group to repeat each line after MC Solomon. Here is this week's couplet:

Your folks are God's guide for you
So listen to their point of view.

Activities

Family role plays

Role plays
10 mins

Split the group into pairs and hand each a slip of paper on which is written one of the followi role play situations. Ask them to put together a role play of the described situation. After five minutes get back together and perform them to each other and perhaps discuss.

- *A couple expecting their first baby discuss the challenge of bringing it up.*
- *Two parents discussing what they will do about their twelve year-old child who is not very happy and whom they suspect is stealing from them.*
- *Two friends talking about their parents. One has 'hard' parents and the other 'soft'.*
- *A thirteen year-old boy/girl discusses the new ground rules now that s/he is a teenager with his/h parents.*
- *A fourteen year-old girl who thinks she might be pregnant finally plucks up courage to tell her mum.*
- *The dad of an unhappy twelve year-old boy is trying to find out what is wrong. (The lad is being bullied at his new school.)*
- *Two mothers chat over a cup of tea about the problems they are having with their teenage daughters.*

Wise and foolish

Enhancing the proverb
5 mins

Split the group into pairs or threes and ask each to make an enhanced audio version of the proverb. They are to read the two halves of the proverb inserting appropriate improvised sound effects and speech to illustrate each. Give them this example and see what they can come up with:

Wise children make their fathers proud of them . . .
applause 'Well done daughter, another trophy to add to the collection!'
Foolish ones bring their mothers grief . . .
police sirens 'Yes officer that is my son. What's he been doing now?' *sniff*

What would you do?

Parent discussion starters
8 mins

The aim of this activity is to help the group to see things from the perspective of the people who look after them. Get them to imagine that they have been left at home to look after a younger brother or sister (aged eight) for the day. Ask them what they would do in the situations listed below. You may well find that there is quite a discrepancy between what the group members would let children in their care do and what they want their own parents or guardians to let them get away with. Pick up on this and discuss it together. (Do be sensitive t the fact that some children might not have both a dad and a mum at home.)

What would the group members do if their little brother or sister . . .
- *Wanted to go out shopping on their own*
- *Wanted you to rent a certificate 15 video for them*
- *Wanted to raid the drinks cupboard*

- *Went out and then didn't return when s/he said s/he would*
- *Broke a window*

Parental perspective

lopes and fears
5 mins

Hand out two slips of paper to each group member and get them to make two lists: one of the hopes that the people bringing them up might have for them and the other of their fears. See the list below for suggestions. Then ask them to ponder how they can be wise towards those who are bringing them up, bearing in mind the proverb and what was said in the 'Parent Interview'. Let this lead into the prayer time.

Hopes
- *that they would be happy*
- *get a good job*
- *good health*
- *love God*
- *find the right partner*

Fears
- *that they might get in with bad company*
- *might get involved with drugs, etc.*
- *might not get on at school/college*
- *might be unhappy*
- *die young*

Bottled prayers

Praying together
4 mins

Make the point that it is wise to try and live in a way that pleases the people who are bringing you up because they are God's gift to us to help us grow up as wise human beings. Hand out slips of paper and encourage the group to either write prayers for the people that bring them up, or asking God to help them be wise towards them. Pass round the prayer bottle so that each person can pray their prayer, either silently or out loud and then bottle it.

Pearls of wisdom

ndering the proverb
2 mins

Hand out bead number seven and get each group member to thread it on their shoe lace or copper wire. Say the proverb together a few times, *'Wise children make their parents proud of them.'* Then run through the other pearls of wisdom together.

Wise Ways with Words

The Aim: To understand that we will have to live with the consequences of wha we say.

The Lightning Bolt: 'You will have to live with the consequences of everythin you say. What you say can preserve life or destroy it; so you must accept the conse quences of your words.' Proverbs 18:20–21

Equipment Check List

PRESENTATIONS

- ❑ theme music
- ❑ 'P on P' tape or video & Wisdometer
- ❑ wisdom bottle and music
- ❑ news theme tune & props
- ❑ Speech-way code OHPs & kit
- ❑ MC Solomon outfit & music

ACTIVITIES

- ❑ paper & pens
- ❑ sets of 'Quotes & Consequences' cards
- ❑ photos of people
- ❑ prayer bottle, paper & pens
- ❑ shoe laces & beads
- ❑ copies of daily readings

Letter to leaders

Words can have extraordinary power for both good and ill. The sage writes that what we say can either preserve life or destroy it so we must accept the consequences of our words. Occasionally Jane and I get into a serious disagreement (mostly sparked off by a bit of map reading). In a heated state like that we can both say things that we don't really mean, but whic are hurtful nonetheless. The strange thing is that the same power of speech is also the means to reconciliation. When we apologise forgiveness and healing come.

Words are rather like a scalpel. In the hands of a wise person they can be used for delicate, essential and life-saving operations. In the hands of a careless or foolish person they can cause untold damage. Like a scalpel, the razor sharp tool of words needs to be handled with care.

- ***How can you become a wiser user of words? Ask God to help you take some concrete steps in that direction.***

- ***Do you need to apologise to anyone for hurting them with your words? Perhaps you could use the power of words to put the situation right?***

It's another viscious word attack!
OK. I've got the KINDWORD kit ready!
AMBULANCE
screech

Presentations

Welcome and introduction

Sparking off
1 min

Have the *Rise Up, Wise Up* theme music playing as the group arrives and give them all a very warm welcome. Introduce the meeting and explain that today's power-packed proverb is all about how to be a wise user of words.

The People on the Pavement

Street wise?
2 mins

Play the clip of tape in which two or three People on the Pavement answer the question, *'H much responsibility should you take for the consequences of what you say?'* Give the group the chance to vote on the wisdom or folly of each answer and declare the result of the vote on Wisdometer.

Message in a bottle

Bottled proverb
2 mins

Switch on the wisdom bottle theme music, unveil the bottle and ask for a volunteer to uncor it, fish out the manuscript and read the proverb, which says: *'You will have to live with the consequences of everything you say. What you say can preserve life or destroy it: so you must accept the consequences of your words.'*

The power of words

5 second sketches
1 min

This is a very simple sketch making the point that words can have a very powerful effect for better or worse. All you require is a telephone, the phone ring sound effects on the audio cassette, and five or six leaders or group members to answer the phone. Each one reacts in very different way to what they hear on the other end. The audience never hears the messa but just sees the character's reaction - either bursting into tears, looking shocked, leaping for joy, smiling, looking relieved, laughing, being angry, etc. As soon as they have put the receive down and reacted to the message, the phone rings again and the next person answers it, and so on.

Here is the news

Word news
3 mins

This news broadcast consists of reports that demonstrate the power of words. Each item concludes with a carefully concealed proverb about the wise use of words. Set up a news de and chair, play the news theme tune on the audio cassette and read the following script in yo own newsreader style.

Good morning. Here is the news with... (your name).

The President of the United States of America, currently under great pressure because of the lawnmower ban, went on an official visit to his old infant school today. He was presented with a large bouquet of flowers by a six year-old student while the whole school sang, 'We love you Mr President'; a song they had especially composed for the occasion. For the first time since the crisis began a smile was seen on the President's face. One of his aides said afterwards (in an American accent), ***'Worry can rob you of happiness, but kind words will cheer you up.'***

The winner of TV's controversial 'Jerk of the Year' award was announced today. It went to red-faced Barry Burchill for his astonishing performance on the 'So Just How Smart Are You?' quiz show. Barry amazed the show's audience by interrupting the question master with his answer to every single question, but failed to get a single question right. Engraved on the Jerk of the Year award were the wise words, ***'Listen before you answer. If you don't you are being stupid and insulting.'*** *Let's hope Barry takes them to heart.*

Earlier today the goalkeeper of premier league football club Rudgewick Rovers was sacked for mouthing off in public about what a sad case the manager was. A Rudgewick Rovers fan who witnessed the incident said, ***'Be careful what you say and protect your life. A careless talker destroys himself.'***

In a speech in the House of Commons the Prime Minister announced his plans for the improvement of provision for cyclists in cities. The speech was universally praised for its clarity and vision. One political commentator said afterwards, ***'An idea well expressed is like a design of gold, set in silver.'***

A housewife from Birmingham, Mrs Ethel Sykes, was rushed to hospital this afternoon after telling her son Trevor that she had prepared a surprise meal for his sixteenth birthday. Her serious injury came about when Trevor said that he'd never inflict his mum's cooking on his mates. A spokesperson for the hospital where Mrs Sykes is being treated said, ***'Thoughtless words can wound as deeply as any sword, but wisely spoken words can heal.'***

And lastly the libel case against the country's most controversial DJ was concluded today. Jonny Blab, accused of destroying the career of the music band 'The Time Warp Wombats' by describing their music as 'rubbish', was found guilty in the High Court today. He was fined £100,000. In his summing up the judge said, ***'What you say can preserve life or destroy it; so you must accept the consequences of your words.'***

That's all for now. Next news at 12 o'clock.

The 'Speech-way Code'

Advice for word users
4 mins

This is a short illustrated broadcast from the Department of Words giving advice on the safe use of words. Photocopy the four illustrations on the following pages onto acetates for use with an OHP. Dress a leader up in some kind of 'Speech-way Code' costume and get them to deliver the following script to the group, whilst displaying the acetates on the OHP.

Words are a great resource and have massive positive potential. However, they can also be dangerous and even lethal, so we in the Department of Words have put together four simple guidelines for users of words. If you follow these tips you will find that your words do more good than harm.

Tip 1.

Always put your brain into gear before opening your mouth. If you don't you may say something you regret later. **cartoon 1** *This is the mistake that Sid makes in this picture. That's not the wa inspire confidence in the girlfriend. Yes, wise word users think before they speak.*

Tip 2.

Before opening up the mouth and pulling away into speech always look round you carefully to ma sure the person you are talking about is not standing behind you. **cartoon 2** *Take the example Alison and Jackie in this picture. They haven't taken the time to look round before speaking out a will soon have a collision with an angry head-teacher. Yes, wise word users make sure they don't speak out into the path of oncoming traffic.*

Tip 3.

Never accelerate too quickly. You may lose control and end up in a smash. That is what is happening in this picture. **cartoon 3** *Sid and Jim have let their words run out of control and the are heading towards a punch up. Yes, wise word users always accelerate steadily.*

Tip 4.

If you feel that you are losing control of your words then immediately perform an emergency stop Stop what you are saying there and then. **cartoon 4** *That is just what Mrs Brown does here. Realising the conversation is getting out of control, she immediately performs an emergency stop, and so gives the situation a chance to cool off.*

So all you word users out there. Remember:

- *Always put your brain into gear before opening your mouth.*
- *Look around carefully before opening the mouth and pulling away.*
- *Never accelerate too quickly.*
- *Perform an emergency stop as soon as you begin to lose control of your words.*

If you follow these four simple tips you will be a wise word user. Have a safe journey through life. Goodbye.

Sing along with Solomon
3 mins

MC Solomon song

MC Solomon takes the group through the first eight weeks of his song. Play the backing beat and get the group to repeat each line after MC Solomon. Here is this week's couplet:

What you say can heal or hurt
So think twice before you blurt.

FWOORACH!! SHE'S A BIT OF ALL RIGHT!

The head is SUCH a JERK!
He is isn't he! PFFTTT !!

What's that you said mate?
I SAID...

Let's talk about it another time, OK?

ctivities

Consequences

A word game
6 mins

Play a game of consequences with the group. Hand each group member a piece of paper and a pen. Get them to write the name of any male character, real or fictitious, at the top of the sheet, fold over the top of the paper so the name is concealed and pass the sheet of paper to the person on their right. Then ask them each to write the word ***'met'*** at the top of their new sheet of paper, followed by the name of a female character, fold over the paper again and pass it on. Next they write the word ***'in'*** followed by the place where the meeting occurred, fold it over and pass it on. Then the words ***'She said to him'*** followed by what she said, fold over and pass it on. Then ***'He said to her'*** followed by what he said, fold over and pass it on. Finally write the words, ***'And the consequence was'*** followed by the chosen consequence. Once each story is completed, pass the paper on once more, and get each person in turn to unfold the stories and read them out. You are likely to get something completely nonsensical but possibly funny, such as:

Bugs Bunny
met ...*my mum*
in ...*the Mediterranean Sea*
She said to him ...*'Have you got the price of a cup of tea?'*
He said to her ...*'I'll huff and I'll puff and I'll blow your house down.'*
And the consequence was ...*spring came early that year.*

Quotes and consequences

Mix & match
5 mins

Divide the group into teams of between two and four. Before the meeting make enough photocopies of the 'Quotes and Consequences' cards on page 103 (enlarge by 141%) for each team to have a set. Cut up each set of twenty cards and put them in an envelope. Explain that you are going to give each team an envelope containing ten cards with quotations that changed the course of history, and ten cards that describe the historical event they changed. They have got to try and match up the words with the events they caused. If you like it could be a race between the teams.

Health warnings

ondering e proverb
10 mins

Read the proverb together, then split the group into pairs or threes and get them to write health warnings for words. These should emphasise the good and bad potential of words and perhaps include some tips on how to handle them wisely. Get back together and read or present these to each other and discuss if appropriate.

Preserved or destroyed?

Newspaper features
10 mins

Split the group into twos or threes and hand each group a photo of a person cut from a magazine. Ask each team to invent a newspaper style story about the person in their picture, and how their life has been either preserved or destroyed by other people's words. Once th have had enough time to write their stories get back together and read them to each other.

For example, here is a story about a man whose life and career were destroyed by someone else's words: *Mr Harry Crate, a wine taster for the prestigious Binnends Wine Company, was unexpectedly suspended from his job last week after allegations were made that he was continua drunk at work. Mr Crate denies this emphatically and believes that these allegations were made a fellow employee jealous of his top job. Mr Crate will not work again until the management has carried out investigations. As this usually takes three to four years Mr Crate's wine tasting skills wi probably 'go off' and he will never work again as a wine taster. THE EDITOR OF 'THE ECHO' DEMANDS JUSTICE AT THE BINNENDS WINE COMPANY NOW. REINSTATE HARRY CRATE!*

Bottled prayers

Praying together
4 mins

Get the group to sit quietly and ponder the way they have used their words in the last 24 hours - the things they have said that have either had a positive or negative effect on others. Perhaps you could give them some examples from your last 24 hours. Then hand out slips of paper and encourage the group to write prayers asking God to help them be wise users of words. Pass the bottle and bottle the prayers.

Pearls of wisdom

Pondering the proverb
2 mins

Hand out the shoe laces or wire and get the group to thread the eighth bead (pearl of wisdom). All say the pearl of wisdom together: *'You will have to live with the consequences of everything you say.'* Then run through the other pearls of wisdom together.

'Drink me!' **Label on a magic bottle**	Caused a 'Wonderland' shrinking experience
'We shall defend our island, whatever the cost may be, we shall fight on the beaches, we shall fight on the landing grounds, we shall fight in the fields, etc. we shall never surrender.' **Winston Churchill**	Helped create the British will to resist Hitler in the Second Word War
'No Albert, you are NOT going into the circus. You're going to be a scientist and that's final.' **Mother Einstein**	The theory of relativity and the nuclear bomb
'The workers have nothing to lose but their chains. They have a world to gain. Workers of the world unite.' **Karl Marx**	The rise of Communism.
'Oooh yes, I really fancy a boat trip!' **Christopher Columbus**	Discovery of the Americas
'And now we will make human beings.' **God**	Us
Pussy said to the owl, *'You elegant fowl! How charmingly sweet you sing! O let us be married, too long we have tarried: But what shall we do for a ring.'*	The first ever animal marriage
'Darling, do get out of my kitchen and do your thinking in the orchard!' **Mrs Newton**	The discovery of the theory of gravity
'Ugg, ur, na, uun.' **Norman the Neanderthal Man**	Communication between human beings
'Hey, give us that pig bladder. I reckons we could have a laff with that.' **Anonymous**	The invention of the game of football

Wisdom on Guard

The Aim: To inspire each other to stay away from the dangerous traps in life.

The Lightning Bolt: 'If you love your life, stay away from the traps that catch the wicked along the way.' Proverbs 22:5

Equipment Check List

PRESENTATIONS
- ❑ theme music
- ❑ pantomime style trap kit
- ❑ 'P on P' tape or video & Wisdometer
- ❑ wisdom bottle & music
- ❑ paper & pens
- ❑ 24 trappability quiz posters
- ❑ mouse sound effects & microphone
- ❑ MC Solomon outfit & music

ACTIVITIES
- ❑ suspicious looking object
- ❑ sweets or matchsticks
- ❑ paper & pens
- ❑ large sheet of paper, magazines, scissors, glue, & copies of mousetrap pic
- ❑ prayer bottle, paper & pens
- ❑ shoe laces & beads
- ❑ copies of daily readings

Letter to leaders

Traps are only dangerous if the bait is attractive to the intended victim. A mouse wouldn't be drawn to step onto the mousetrap if the bait was a can of lager. Cheese is what will draw the mouse to take the deadly step. Traps are very personal things. What is one person's trap won' pose the slightest risk to another. So we need to be alert to the traps that we are at risk of falling into, whatever they might be.

You may be surprised to read that in today's proverb the sage doesn't advise us to 'resist' the traps we find tempting. He tells us to 'avoid' them all together. This may sound like splitting hairs but, to pursue the silly example, it has got to be easier for the mouse to avoid the mousetrap altogether than resist the urge to eat the cheese when it's only a sniff away.
This is a message that will be very hard for our young people to put into practice. The other day I was talking to a friend who has teenage children about the traps that face young people today; experimenting with soft drugs for example. He compared growing up as a teenager to walking down a corridor. When he was young people took drugs behind the closed doors tha lined the corridor. But now, not only are the doors wide open, but people stand in the corrid and try to drag passers-by into the side rooms. The traps that young people face today are much harder to avoid than those young people faced just ten years ago. We need to understand that and give them lots more encouragement and support.

- ***Think about your group members and the traps they face each day. Pray that Go will give each of them the will to avoid the traps that threaten them.***

Don't touch it!
It's a TRAP!!
Can't see
any risks
myself.

Presentations

Welcome and introduction

Sparking off
1 min

Play the *Rise Up, Wise Up* theme music as the group arrives and give them a warn welcome. Introduce the subject of the ninth *Rise Up, Wise Up* meeting—traps and how to avoid them. Then go on to lay a pantomime style trap for one of the leaders who is apparently late. Perh a small plastic bowl of water positioned over the door (or some other joke shop trick). Seco later the late leader rushes through the door apologising for being late and spectacularly falls i the trap.

The People on the Pavement

Street wise?
2 mins

Play the clip of tape in which two or three People on the Pavement answer the question *'W traps in life are there for people to fall into?'* After each answer give the group the chance to v on the wisdom or folly of each and declare the result on the Wisdometer.

Message in a bottle

Bottled proverbs
2 mins

Switch on the bottled wisdom theme music and unveil the wisdom bottle. Ask for a voluntee to open the bottle, fish out the manuscript and read the proverb, *'If you love your life, stay aw from the traps that catch the wicked along the way.'*

Guess the trap

The trapped speak out
5 mins

Get a range of characters to read out one of the following statements about a trap they have fallen into. The statement doesn't actually specify what the trap is and the group members hav try and work it out from what **is** said. Hand out slips of paper and pens, so the group member can note down what they think each trap is. Once you have finished all five statements get the group to say what they thought each trap was, then run through the correct answers.

Trap 1: *Well, the problems really began when my mum and dad brought me my own personal c for Christmas. I enjoyed using the one at school you see, and they thought it would be good for m to have one all to myself. At first everything was fine; nothing more than a hobby. But then as I g better, it used to take up more and more of my time. I was in another world. More fun than the real one. I would be lost for hours. It wasn't long before I stopped going out with my friends and started staying up late and the rest of my life just took the back seat.* **(Computer addict)**

Trap 2: *I've always been like this. But recently things have been getting a lot worse. At school I never volunteer for anything in case I mess it up - I'd be so embarrassed. I don't really like going o to parties because I'm never sure if I'm wearing the right kind of clothes. I wouldn't like people to laugh at me. I expect you think I'm really silly being like this. But I feel much safer not taking any risks. I'm fine when I'm at home, except when my brother has his friends round. When they're th I tend to stay in my room because I don't want to get in their way.* **(Worrying what others think of you)**

Trap 3: *It all started one day at school. I was with my mates behind the bike sheds when one of them started sharing some round. I didn't want to try one but I thought they'd think I was a wimp to say no. After the first one I couldn't really see what the big deal was, but it became a habit, mainly because it was fun doing something secretly together. My dad would hit the roof if he knew, which is really hypocritical considering I know he has a few in the pub.* **(Smoking)**

Trap 4: *It all started when I suddenly realised that I wasn't really prepared for the big day. I'd been too busy playing football. Then I had the brainwave: I could probably get by if I wrote down a few key facts and kept them in my pencil case. No one noticed and it worked a treat, and so I did the same thing next time. I thought up all sorts of clever plans; using invisible writing on my notepad, the discreet over the shoulder glance, and for really desperate cases, a trip to the toilet. I must have the knack because I haven't been caught yet. You call it a trap but it suits me fine.* **(Cheating)**

Trap 5: *I think I first fell into this trap when I was very young and never really realised that it was a trap at all. I was just doing what came naturally. At first it was things like being bad tempered when someone wanted to play with my toys, and making sure I got mummy's attention before my brother and sister. Then it was things like fixing it so that we always watched the TV programmes I wanted. Basically I thought I had the right to have a good time.* **(Selfishness)**

Your personal trappability rating

***ctive self-
ssessment***
6 mins

Take 24 large pieces of paper (about A3). In very large writing number the first nineteen 1–19 and the last five A–E. Then write out the following questions under the appropriate number or letter. Pin these up at eye level on the walls of your meeting room. Pin up sheets A-E in the four corners of the room and by the door.

Explain to the group that they are about to go on a quest to discover just how trappable they are. Ask them to start at 'box one' and answer the question 'yes' or 'no'. At the bottom of each sheet they will be told which box to go to next, e.g. **Yes⇨ box 3 No⇨ box 2.** Once they have been to between six and nine boxes they will be sent to box A, B, C, D or E. This is their trappability rating. Once they have read their rating and their 'trappability tip' they should sit down by the box, and wait for the others to finish. If you have a large group then you may need to start them off on the quest in staggered groups.

The Questions

1. If your younger brother or sister asked if they could borrow your new personal stereo or computer game would you let them? **Yes⇨ box 3 No⇨ box 2**

2. You've just started at a new school. You want to get in with the lads/girls, but you've got to nick something from the corner shop before they'll let you into their group. Would you do it? **Yes⇨ box 6 No⇨ box 3**

3. That particularly annoying person in your class has just done something unbelievably stupid. Would you tell your mates about it and have a laugh? **Yes⇨ box 7 No⇨ box 4**

4. Have you brought a lottery ticket, or got someone to buy one for you in the last month? **Yes⇨ box 8 No⇨ box 5**

5. Are you always polite to the canteen staff at school? **Yes⇨ box 9 No⇨ box 8**

6. Have you hit anyone in anger in the last two weeks? **Yes⇨ box 10 No⇨ box 11**

7. You want to go out for the evening with your mates but you know your mum won't let y
till you've done your homework. Would you tell a white lie if you knew you could get away with it? **Yes➪ box 6 No➪ box 11**

8. If you were invited to watch an 18 certificate video at a friend's house, would you go? **Yes➪ box 7 No➪ box 11**

9. You're on the school bus when the 'sad case' of the class chokes on his/her lunch. Would you snigger or laugh? **Yes➪ box 11 No➪ box 12**

10. Have you got drunk with your friends in the last month? **Yes➪ box 13 No➪ box 14**

11. You are sitting next to the class star pupil in a test and find that you can easily see their ex
paper. Would you take any tips from their answers? **Yes➪ box 14 No➪ box 15**

12. If a beginner thrashed you at your favourite sport or computer game would it put you in foul mood? **Yes➪ box 15 No➪ box 16**

13. Has anyone who knows you well called you lazy recently? **Yes: ➪ box 17 No➪ box 1**

14. You're Christmas shopping with your mates and see a fortune teller's caravan in the precinct. One of your friends wants to get their palm read. Would you get yours read too? **Yes➪ box 13 No ➪ box 18**

15. Do you ever cheer when you see violence on telly? **Yes➪ box 18 No➪ box 19**

16. If a member of the year above made a rude comment about what you were wearing, would you wear that outfit again in public? **Yes➪ box E, No➪ box 19**

17. You are at a party where soft drugs are being used. Your mates are doing it. Would you? **Yes➪ box A No➪ box 18**

18. Have you deliberately done or said anything to hurt another member of your class in the last month? **Yes➪ box B No➪ box C**

19. Have you smoked a cigarette in the last week? **Yes➪ box C No➪ box D**

A. Trappability Rating: Easy Meat: *When it comes for falling for the big traps in life - you'v got style. You take the bait without even spotting the danger. O trappable one, you need to chang you trappitude fast or before you know it you will be trap-trap-trapped for good.*

B. Trappability Rating: Heading for Captivity: *Be warned! Captivity looms if you don't st steering clear of some of those traps that you find so tempting. If you value your life then make a concerted effort to resist that tasty looking, but terrible bait.*

C. Trappability Rating: Trap Casual: *I'm sorry to say that your attitude to the traps in life i touch on the casual side. You avoid the trap if it suits you, but if the bait looks tasty enough you w take it without batting an eye lid. If you want to stay free then try a bit harder to stay away from those traps that are most tempting to you.*

D. Trappability Rating: Trap Wary: *Your record on steering clear of the traps in life is not b in fact you are at the wiser end of the trappability scale. But you do fall for some of them, and all traps are potentially dangerous. So keep your eyes wide open, and renew your efforts to keep your freedom.*

E. Trappability Rating: Trap Proof (almost): *Well, no one's going to trap you if you can h it. Well done, O wise one. But beware of the trap of overconfidence or pride. The deadliest of the all!*

A mouse message

word from ond the trap
3 mins

Explain to the group that you are about to conduct an interview with a mouse now in the great skirting board in the sky. You need the mouse sound effects on the audio cassette, a translator and an interviewer. Here is a rough script to work round:

Interviewer	*(to audience)* We have on the audio satellite link a mouse who has experienced the terminal trauma of being caught by a mousetrap. As I don't speak 'Mouse' we are going to use a translator to conduct the interview. Hello, Mr Mouse!
Translator	Eek eeek
Mouse	*(play I sec of mouse sound effects on tape)*
Translator	He says hello.
Interviewer	Mr Mouse, we'll get straight to the point. I believe that you have something that you really want to tell the members of this youth group?
Translator	Eek eeek eeekeeekkk eeek.
Mouse	*(taped mouse sound effects)*
Translator	He says that he would like to give the group a warning about the danger of traps *(more taped mouse)*. He feels that no one ever warned him and he paid the ultimate price for his ignorance *(tape)*. This is what happened. He had just moved into a new house with his wife and micelets *(tape)*. As he left his hole to search for food one night he noticed a large contraption near the entrance to their family hole *(tape)*. On it was the most delicious looking lump of cheese he had ever seen *(tape)*. It was enough to feed the family for a week *(tape)*. As soon as he stepped onto the wooden object—WHAM! *(tape)* The next thing he knew he was in the great skirting board in the sky *(tape)*. And his poor wife and micelets were left all alone in the world.
Interviewer	*(sniff)* How terrible! How very tragic… So how might things have been different if you had known?
Translator	Eeeek eek eek e eeekeeek?
Mouse	*(taped mouse sound effects)*
Translator	He says that if he had received a decent education in traps he would easily have been able to identify the contraption for what it really was—a mousetrap! *(tape)* He wouldn't have taken the bait... He wouldn't have fallen for the tasty cheese ploy... *(tape)* He wouldn't have been tricked... And his wife and micelets wouldn't now be fatherless.
Interviewer	Sniff. So Mr Mouse what is the message in this for us here today?
Translator	Eeek eek eeeek?
Mouse	*(taped mouse sound effects)*
Translator	He says that if we value our lives, if we care about ourselves and those we love *(tape)* we must, must, must learn to identify the dangerous traps that are out there waiting to get us *(tape)*. And we must steer clear of them. Don't go anywhere near—even if they do look so very tasty (like the cheese) *(tape)*. It's a TRAP and it could be fatal. It is too late for him but it is not too late for us.
Interviewer	Mr Mouse, thank you so much for telling us your tragic tale. We will take your warning to heart, and we will pass it on to others. Thank you so much.
Translator	Eeeekk eeekeeeeke eeeke.
Mouse	*(taped mouse sound effects)*
Translator	He says thank you and goodbye.

MC Solomon Song

Sing along with Solomon
3 mins

MC Solomon takes the group through the first nine weeks of his song. Play the backing beat and get the group to repeat each line after MC Solomon. Here is this week's couplet:

If about your life you care
Stay away from trap and snare.

Activities

Trappable?

A trick
2 mins

Start off by making an obviously suspicious offer to the group. For example, produce a black bin liner and promise to give fifty pence to anyone who puts their hand in the bin liner and takes out an item. If you behave suspiciously enough (holding the bin liner gingerly away from your body and whispering to the other leaders) you hopefully won't get any takers. If so, ask them why? Did they smell a trap per chance?

Yes no black white

A game
5 mins

Give each group member five matchsticks or small sweets and explain that they have to try and win sweets off everyone else by tricking them into saying either YES, NO, BLACK or WHITE. They can do this by asking questions such as, 'Have you got any brothers?' Each time someone says one of the forbidden words they have to hand over a sweet. The winner is the one with most at the end. (The point here is that the devil tries to trick us into making mistakes, and when we fall for it we lose out. If we are wise we will be one step ahead of him!)

The trap challenge

trap tasks
10 mins

This is a contest in which teams have to complete a series of tasks on the trap theme. Split the group into teams of about four. Spread the teams round the room and then give them the following tasks to complete, awarding points arbitrarily (1,000 here, and 54 million there) and fixing it so that it ends up as a draw.

- In 60 seconds write a dictionary definition of the word 'trap'.
- Improvise a conversation between two mice discussing whether to eat the cheese on that strange contraption on the floor (mousetrap).
- Build a 'youth group leader trap' from the bodies of your team members and demonstrate how it works.
- Complete the following limerick on the theme of the lure of the trap (note: 'chap' rhymes with 'trap'): *There once was a foolish young chap...*

The lure of the trap

collage & discussion
10 mins

Take a large sheet of paper or card and draw a road wiggling its way all over the page. Make ten or fifteen photocopies of the picture of the mousetrap on page 113 and stick them at various places by the side of the road. Show the picture to the group and then read the proverb together. Then hand out some scissors, colour magazines and newspapers. Ask them to cut out words or images of the kind of things that they consider to be human equivalents of the cheesy bait on the mouse traps. Get them to stick these pictures on the mouse traps. Develop this into a discussion about the traps that they face and practical ways of steering clear of them.

Problem pages

Advice for the trapped
10 mins

All of us are bound to make mistakes and fall into traps occasionally. So what should we do then? This activity gets the group members to write problem page answers to people who have fallen into one of a range of traps.

Write out the following 'professions' and 'traps' on separate slips of paper. Put the 'professio in one bag or hat and the 'traps' in another. Split the group into pairs and ask each pair to pi 'profession' slip and a 'trap' slip. Hand out sheets of paper and pens and ask them to imagine that they are agony aunts that have just received a letter from the person described on their 'profession' slip. Their correspondent has fallen into the trap described on the other slip. Ask them to write a suitable reply to their troubled correspondent. Do encourage them to write positive answers. Once they have had time to do this get back together and ask them to rea them out.

PROFESSIONS
- *Train Driver*
- *Athlete*
- *School girl*
- *Teacher*
- *Politician*
- *Football player*
- *The Queen*
- *Vicar*
- *Granny*
- *Pet shop assistant*

TRAPS
- *Cheating*
- *Stealing*
- *Swearing*
- *Laziness*
- *Gossiping*
- *Watching too much TV*
- *Lying*
- *Being selfish*
- *Being spiteful*
- *Greed*

Bottled prayers

Praying together
4 mins

Remind the group of the traps on the picture and encourage them to write prayers asking G to help them stay away from the traps that threaten them. Perhaps you could tell the group about a trap that you have to try and avoid and how God helps you. This might help them t take it seriously and be more honest. Once everyone is ready pass the bottle and bottle the prayers.

Pearls of wisdom

Pondering the proverbs
5 mins

Hand out the shoe laces or wire and get the group to thread the ninth bead (pearl of wisdo All say the pearl of wisdom together: *'If you love your life, stay away from the traps that catch wicked along the way.'* Then run through the other pearls of wisdom together.

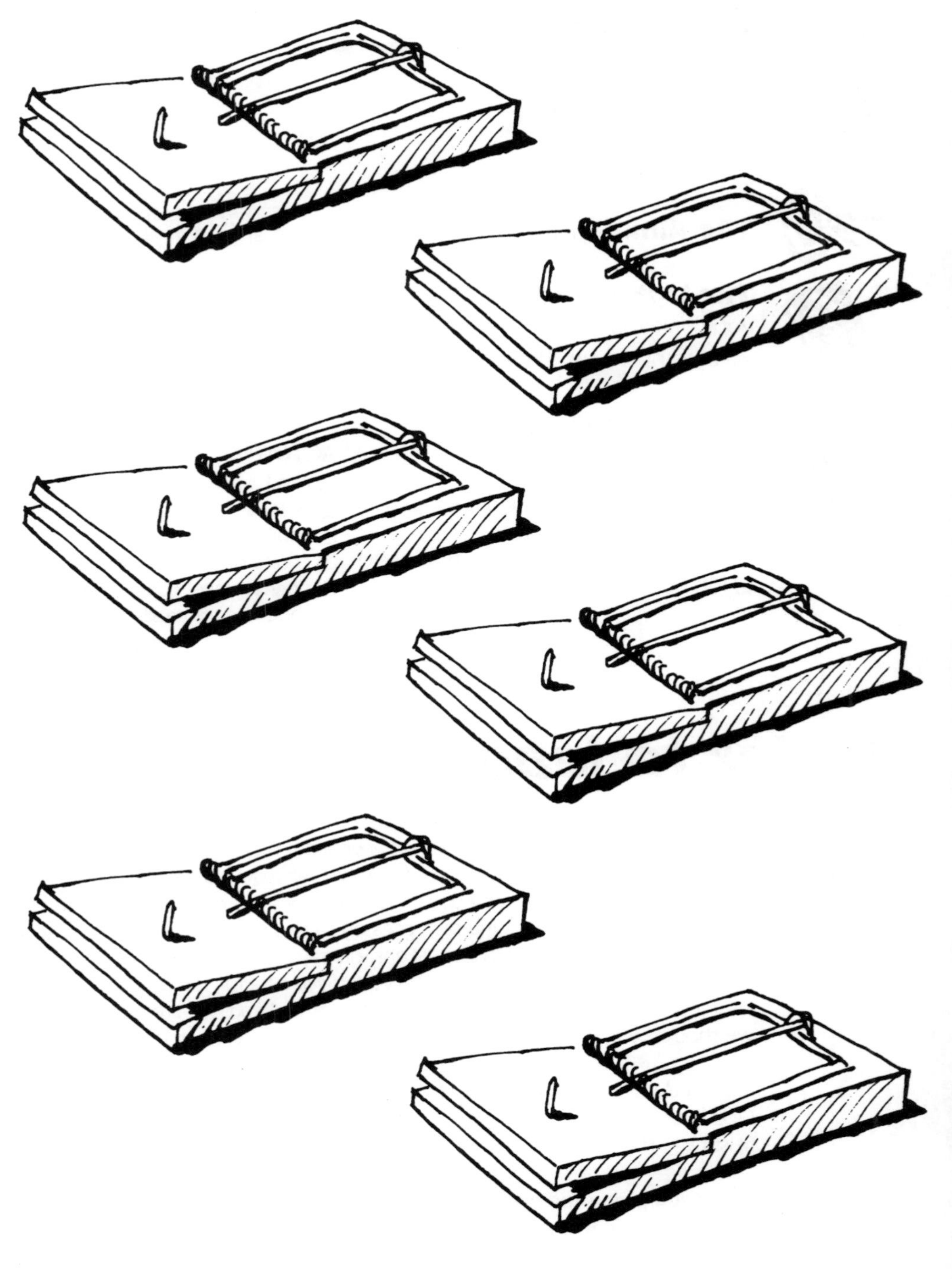

The Trust of the Wise

The Aim: To understand that it is wise to trust God in all situations.

The Lightning Bolt: 'Trust in the Lord with all your heart. Never rely on wh you think you know. Remember the Lord in everything you do, and he will show you the right way.' Proverbs 3:5–6

Equipment Check List

PRESENTATIONS
- ❑ theme music
- ❑ 'P on P' tape or video & Wisdometer
- ❑ wisdom bottle and music
- ❑ costumes for 'Things people trust' sketch
- ❑ MC Solomon outfit & music

ACTIVITIES
- ❑ blind fold & obstacle course
- ❑ post cards, magazines, glue, etc.
- ❑ paper & pens
- ❑ copies of 'Trusting God' assessment quiz
- ❑ prayer bottle, paper & pens
- ❑ shoe laces & beads
- ❑ bucket containing quiz question slips
- ❑ copies of daily readings

Letter to leaders

I don't think we are ever likely to get a better explanation of what a relationship with God is about than this: *'Trust in the Lord with all your heart. Never rely on what you think you know. Remember the Lord in everything you do, and he will show you the right way.'* True faith is abou trusting God. Sadly, however, I don't find that comes too naturally. How can I learn to trust h more? Well, in verses 9-12 the sage goes on to give some practical clues as to what this trus should mean in two contrasting situations. He says that when life is going well we should tru God by giving away the best of our harvest of good things, rather than hoarding them as an insurance policy for the future. When, on the other hand, we are going through a rough pat we should be open to the possibility that God is trying to teach us something.

It is a circle of ever increasing trust and proven trustworthiness. The more we try to involve God in our lives, the better we get to know him. The more we know him, the easier it is to trust him. The more we trust him, the more we involve him, and so on.

- ***Are you giving the cycle of increasing trust and proven trustworthiness a chance start spinning? If not, what can you do to start it off?***

Presentations

Welcome and introduction

Sparking off
1 min

Have the *Rise Up, Wise Up* theme music playing as the group arrives and give them a warm welcome. Introduce the theme of the final *Rise Up, Wise Up* meeting - the wisdom of trusting God.

The People on the Pavement

Street wise?
2 mins

Play the clip of tape in which two or three of the People on the Pavement answer the question 'What do you think it means to trust in God?' Get the group to vote on whether each answer is wise or foolish and reveal their verdict on the Wisdometer.

Message in a bottle

Bottled wisdom
2 mins

Play the wisdom bottle theme music and unveil the bottle itself. Ask for a volunteer to uncork it, fish out the manuscript and read the ancient words of wisdom from King Solomon: *'Trust in the Lord with all your heart. Never rely on what you think you know. Remember the Lord in everything you do, and he will show you the right way.'*

The things people trust

A sketch
3 mins

Explain to the group that when it comes to finding something to trust in life then God is the only truly reliable option. People do of course put their trust in other things, but usually with not very consistent results. To make this point perform the following short sketch in which a character (Jo), who is searching for something to trust in life, gets conflicting advice from people he (or she) meets at the bus stop. Do change the characters as you see fit. They could even be played by the same person wearing different hats.

City Gent Good morning, sir. Where are you off to today?

Jo Ah, well, I've been thinking about my life and how what I need is something reliable to depend on. Something solid that I can trust. So I'm off to get myself a dog. Man's best friend!

City Gent Ahhh no! You don't want to get yourself a dog. Bad mistake. I used to have a dog. And I trusted it with all my heart. And then it went and died on me. Unreliable dogs are. If you want something reliable to trust then you should get yourself a good job; sound job, bring in the money. Job for life. That's the way.

Jo Oh right! Thanks mate! *(exit City Gent, enter Cleaner)*

Cleaner Good morning, my luv. Where's you off to today?

Jo Ah, well, I've been thinking about my life and how what I need is something reliable to depend on. Something solid that I can trust. So I'm off to get myself a good job for life. Bring in the money!

Cleaner Ooohh no! I don't thinks you should do that, my dear. Get yourself a by all means, but don't make the mistake of thinking you can trust you job for life. You never know what your employer might do. I had wha thought was a job for life and then I got the sack. Look luv, if you war something reliable to trust in life then follow my advice and get yours some good friends. You can trust your friends - they'll never let you down.

Jo Oh right! Thanks! *(exit Cleaner, enter Teacher)*

Teacher Good morning! Where are you going today?

Jo Ah, well, I've been thinking about my life and how what I need is som thing reliable to depend on. Something solid that I can trust. So I'm of get myself some good friends. You see, your friends will never let you down!

Teacher Oh I say, you mustn't do that. Look, friends are all right, but they'll sti you down. I used to have some friends - stuck together like glue - bu when I went through a bad patch with the old money trouble, couldr see them for dust. My dear chap, if you're looking for something to tr in life, listen to my advice; forget friends, but get yourself a good educ tion. Then you can trust in yourself! In your own brain power.

Jo Oh right! Thanks! *(exit Teacher, enter Traveller)*

Traveller Hiya there. Where you off to today, man?

Jo Ah, well, I've been thinking about my life and how what I need is som thing reliable to depend on. Something solid that I can trust. So I'm of get myself a good education. Get my brain in tip top condition, then I' be able to trust myself and my own intelligence!

Traveller Hey man, I should back off there you know; a good education is not a that it's cracked up to be. However much you educate your brain, it's still just your brain. You can't trust a lump of grey matter. I had a good education at *(name a local school)* but I still went the wrong way in life Until I discovered my own cosmology, man. If you want something to rely on then get in touch with your cosmic alignments. You know, you stars. Get yourself a good horoscope and tune in man. I tell you, if yo trust in your stars they won't let you down.

Jo Oh right! Thanks! *(exit Traveller, enter Postman)*

Postman All right mate! Where are you off to today?

Jo Ah, well, I've been thinking about my life and how what I need is som thing reliable to depend on. Something solid that I can trust. So I'm off get in touch with my own cosmic alignments—you know—my horoscope. You see, if you trust in your stars they won't let you down!

Postman No, no, that's a load of old rubbish. It's just mumbo jumbo. I used to into that stuff, but every time I read my stars they always said somethir totally different. And what they said never happened. It's a joke. Just forget it. *(exit)*

Jo *(in despair)* Well, if I can't trust a dog, and I can't trust a good job and money, and I can't trust my friends and I can't trust my brain power or myself, and I can't trust my horoscope, what can I rely on?

Look God, before I trust you I'd like a look at your track record...

Can God be trusted?

A talk demo
3 mins

Explain to the group that when deciding whether to trust a person or a thing we all apply 'the test of experience'. To demonstrate this ask the group some of the following questions. When they answer do challenge them and try and get them to be more specific.

- *Has anyone flown in an aeroplane recently? Why did you get into that enormous lump of metal and trust it to carry you safely through the air at X thousand feet and back to earth again?*
- *Has anyone been to see a doctor or dentist recently? Why did you trust them to give you the right treatment and not carry out some horrible experiment on you?*
- *Has anyone eaten any food in the last 24 hours? Why did you take the risk of eating something that could be highly poisonous?*
- *Has anyone crossed a bridge recently? Why did you take the risk of walking across a contraption that could suddenly collapse and send you plummeting to your death?*

Go on to say that we all use our past experiences to decide whether or not to trust someone or something. The reason that we do trust aeroplanes, doctors, food, and bridges is that in the past they have proved to be trustworthy well over 99.9% of the time. They have passed the 'test of experience' for us and other people. Conclude by making the point that the same principle applies to trusting God: over the years millions and millions of people have found him to be 100 per cent trustworthy. And that is why it is safe for us to trust him today. God's complete trustworthiness passes the sterling test of experience.

On the spot

An interview
3 mins

Interview a youth group leader or member of the church for two or three minutes about how they know God is trustworthy and what it means to trust him. Make sure you ask very practical questions about the reality of trusting God when things go both well and badly. Don't let them get away with waffle. Here are some questions you might like to work round.

- *What was your favourite pastime when you were twelve?*
- *How did you come to discover that God loved you?*
- *If someone wanted to know what evidence you had for believing that God was trustworthy what would you say?*
- *Could you give us an example of a time when you had to trust God in a bad situation? What happened?*
- *What does it mean to trust God when things are going well?*

MC Solomon song

Sing along with Solomon
3 mins

MC Solomon takes the group through the full MC Solomon song. Play the backing beat and get the group to repeat each line after MC Solomon. Here is the final couplet:

There's one final thing to say:
Trust in God come what may.

ctivities

Trust games

rust me?
4 mins

Depending on how much time and space you have play one of the following trust games. Afterwards discuss the following questions:

- *What did it feel like having to trust your guide/catcher?*
- *Were the guides/catchers trustworthy?*
- *What did it feel like being trusted?*
- *Who do you trust most in the world and why? (Mums are a hot favourite here.)*

1. Falling Backwards: Ask for a volunteer and get them to stand with their back to you about one metre away. Explain that you want them to fall backwards without bending their legs and that you will catch them before they hit the floor. (Please make sure you do.) Once they have done this see if anyone else wants to try it.

2. Obstacle course: Set up an obstacle course round the room using chairs, tables, people, balloons, etc. Ask for two volunteers. Blindfold one with a T-towel and ask the other to guide them through the course, either by leading them by the hand or by giving spoken directions. An alternative would be to split the whole group into pairs, one blindfolded and one not, and lead them out of the room, round the outside of the building and back again. You will need to supervise this very carefully. Once you are all back let the pairs swap over, so everyone has a go at both leading and being led.

Trusting God?

ostcards
10 mins

Read the proverb together, then hand out some plain postcards, magazines, scissors, glue and pens, etc. Encourage each group member to make a 'trust in the Lord' postcard with text and images cut from the magazines. Hand out envelopes and get them to address them to themselves. Collect the envelopes and cards in, then during the following week swap the envelopes and cards around and post them. Each group member will then get a special mid-week reminder to trust God.

God's track record on trust

ist contest
6 mins

Split into teams and give each team four minutes to produce as long a list as they can of incidents in the Bible where God proved to be trustworthy. Get back together, go through the lists and see who has the longest list of valid examples. Conclude by making the point that God's track record on trustability is pretty impressive, because he is trustworthy and loving by nature.

Q1. If your mates kept telling you that you were dead ugly what would you think?

❏ *a. Complete tosh! I'm the most good looking guy/girl in the universe. They're just green with envy.*
❏ *b. Oh God, I wish you'd perform a miracle and turn me from an ugly duckling to a beautiful swan.*
❏ *c. I know it's true and I've had enough of their taunts. Life's not worth living any more.*
❏ *d. Sniff, sniff. Well, I can't help the way I look. I know God still loves me whatever they say.*

Q2. How much of your pocket money do you give to charity?

❏ *a. Give to charity! You think I haven't got anything better to do with hard earned cash!*
❏ *b. More than 1/10th regularly each week.*
❏ *c. I don't need to give any because God knows that everything I've got is his anyway.*
❏ *d. The odd few coins now and then when I feel like it.*

Q3. You're delighted to have been invited to the party of a lifetime. You are just getting ready to go out when a friend phones in tears because his/her hamster has died and wants you to come round. What would you do?

❏ *a. Explain that you can't possibly come as you are already going out for the evening.*
❏ *b. Chat to them on the phone for half an hour and then go to the party.*
❏ *c. Phone the party holder, explain that you can't come, then go and spend the evening with the hamsterless friend.*
❏ *d. Go to the party having told them to pull themselves together and to trust God.*

Q4. You have to go into hospital to have your appendix out. How would you react?

❏ *a. Start praying that the appendix would get better so that you don't need the dreaded operation.*
❏ *b. Total panic - shaking all over - general hysterics.*
❏ *c. No worries - piece of cake - take it all in your stride - give me an operation any day. Good laff.*
❏ *d. Be a bit nervous, tell God how you feel and then try not to worry about it.*

Q5. You've just been told that your mum or dad has got a new job which means the family moving to a new area. What would you think as you lay in bed that night?

❏ *a. I don't want to move, but I suppose something good might come out of it. At least Mum's got a better job.*
❏ *b. I'm not going, I'm definitely not going!*
❏ *c. Sniff, sniff.*
❏ *d. Hooray. I'll be getting out of this dump at last. I've packed my bags and I'm ready to go!*

Q6. You have been praying for your Dad to become a Christian. Nothing much seems to be happening. What would you think?

❏ *a. Oh dear. Perhaps God doesn't want my Dad to become a Christian anyway.*
❏ *b. If I've prayed the prayer once, it will happen one day! No need to pray again!*
❏ *c. Oh well, I'll just keep praying till I see some results.*
❏ *d. Huh! I never thought it would work anyway.*

Q7. You have just started at a new school and everything is going really badly; you're struggling to make friends, your struggling with the work, and struggling to cope. What would you say to God about it?

❏ *a. God, ZAP everyone at school, so things get better for me, and do it tomorrow!*
❏ *b. Oh God, I don't like this very much, but I know you're still there. Help me learn something from this hassle.*
❏ *c. Nothing (What's the point?)*
❏ *d. This is another fine mess you've got me into. How about doing something for me for a change?*

Q8. You've just been appointed head boy/girl. What would you write in your diary that night?

❏ *a. 'Well, God I'm really chuffed, but please don't let it go to my head. And please help me to do my best.'*
❏ *b. 'Right! Now we'll get this school sorted out. Boy o boy, are standards going to improve now I'm in charge.'*
❏ *c. 'I've got a funny feeling God might be behind this. Well, if he is I jolly well hope he is going to help me.'*
❏ *d. 'Been appointed head boy/girl. Will turn down the offer tomorrow as I'm not up to the job.'*

Q9. How would your react if you felt that God wanted you to ask your friends to your youth group?

❏ *a. 'Hang on a tick. That's taking this Christianity business a bit far.'*
❏ *b. 'I know it's a good idea, but I'm too shy to ask so I'll pray for them instead.'*
❏ *c. 'That sounds like a good idea, God. Now, which meeting do you think I should ask them to?'*
❏ *d. 'Yes! Next time I see them, I'll grab them by the throat and tell them the good news about Jesus. And who cares if they think I'm weird.'*

Q10. You've gone to stay with an elderly relative for the weekend in her slightly spooky house. You're woken up in the night by a strange noise. What would you do?

❏ *a. Jump out of bed, turn on the lights, and start reading bits of the Bible out loud at the top of your voice, to fend off foul fiends.*
❏ *b. Lie there in terror hoping whatever it was didn't see you.*
❏ *c. Turn over and go back to sleep. Probably just the branches blowing against the window.*
❏ *d. Start praying, then turn on the lights and hope it isn't a werewolf.*

Now add up your scores and find out how much you trust God

1	a3	b1	c0	d2
2	a0	b2	c3	d1
3	a0	b1	c2	d3
4	a1	b0	c3	d2
5	a2	b0	c1	d3
6	a1	b3	c2	d0
7	a3	b2	c0	d1
8	a2	b3	c1	d0
9	a0	b1	c2	d3
10	a3	b0	c2	d1

Desperate Doubter
(0-5)
Judging by the way you answered this quizlet you find it hard to believe that God can be trusted at all. Well, the good news is that he most definitely can! You're not out there all on your own. Take a look around you and see what God's doing for other people and reach out to him yourself. He won't let you down. Promise!

Trust Tentative
(6-13)
Although you're not as trustless as some doubting souls we happen to know, I have to tell you that God is a lot more trustworthy than you think. I mean he's not supreme being of the universe for nothing. So ponder it for a bit and try and relax about those situations that are out of your control and trust him to look after you. He can handle it!

Trust Wise
(14-24)
Well, you must be commended, my friend. Your attitude in life is most definitely sound. You've twigged the fact that God can be depended on and have struck a happy balance between getting on with the job in hand and trusting God in the situations that are beyond your control. You're doin' fine!

Head in the Clouds
(25-30)
You are indeed a most trusting soul, but I'm sorry to say that you place most of your trust in your own wonderful talents and not in God. While we don't want you to start hanging your head in shame, it might be a good idea to take a realistic look at yourself and try and be, dare I say it, a little less arrogant. Remember it's foolish to try and boss God around but it's wise to remember he's the boss. Now have you got that? Well, let's see some action for a change.

Look God, before I trust you I'd like a look at your track record.

So just how much do you trust God?

Turn the page, answer the questions and find out.

How just much do you trust God?

A self-assessment quiz
7 mins

Photocopy (enlarged by 141%) the two sides of the 'So just how much do you trust God?' se assessment quiz on pages 120 and 121. Fold each copy twice so it makes a tall slim leaflet. Gi each member a copy, along with a pen and ask them to complete it and tot up their score. If you feel it's appropriate go on to discuss some of the questions together.

Bottled prayers

Praying together
3 mins

Hand out slips of paper and encourage the group to write prayers thanking God that he's 100% trustworthy. Pass the prayer bottle so that everyone can pray their prayer either out lo or silently and bottle it.

Pearls of wisdom

Pondering the proverbs
3 mins

For the last time remind the group that the proverbs you are looking at this term are like pear of wisdom to be treasured. Hand out the last bead and get them to add it to their shoe lace. Get every one to hold the last bead and say together, *'Trust in the Lord with all your heart.'* Th go back to bead one and work through all ten proverbs. Don't forget to let them take their pearls of wisdom home with them at the end.

End of course quiz

Recap time
10 mins

Run an end of course quiz. Thirty questions are suggested below but do add your own. Split into two teams and run the quiz as a game of football. Write out all the questions on slips of paper and put them in a bucket. Toss a coin to see who kicks off. The team that wins the toss picks a question from the bucket, reads it out and the first team to answer correctly keeps or gains possession of the ball (bucket). A team answering three questions correctly in a row scores a goal.

1. ***How did King Solomon become so wise?***
   God gave him wisdom.
2. ***Name two of the ways Eric the Armadillo tried to be wise?***
   Hard work, street wise, worldly wise, wisdom of old age, seeking God's gift.
3. ***What is the most important thing you can do in life?***
   Seek God's wisdom.
4. ***Complete the verse, 'Wisdom will be your reward...'***
   'If you have reverence for the Lord.'
5. ***Give two good reasons why it's wise to have reverence for God.***
   Name any two of God's attributes: love, power, holiness, infinite, etc. (see pages 36–37
6. ***What is 'reverence'?***
   A feeling or attitude of profound respect (for God).
7. ***Name three types of fool.***
   Gullible, Angry, Know-it-All, Lazy, Smashed, Want-More, Troublemaker, Gossip-Liar.
8. ***What was the message of Inspector Wise?***
   Watch out that you don't become a fool.

9. ***Which fool had the motto, 'Oh, I'll just have ten more minutes in bed'?***
Mr Lazy.

10. ***What should you do 'whenever you possibly can'?***
Good to those who need it.

11. ***How did Dr Wise advise Miss Good to exercise her heart?***
By doing good to other people.

12. ***Who were put on trial?***
People charged with the offence of 'Withholding help from persons in a state of need.'

13. ***What should you tie round your neck?***
Loyalty (and faithfulness).

14. ***Name two parts of the body that were pointed out in the 'Anatomy of Loyalty'.***
Heart, ears, lips, shoulder, hands, feet, (see pages 69–71)

15. ***What was the wise lesson that we can learn from dogs?***
Loyalty.

16. ***What shapes your life?***
Your thoughts.

17. ***What happens if you plant generous thoughts?***
You get generous actions. (What you plant is what you get, see page 78.)

18. ***What 'cause of death' did the post mortem reveal?***
A nasty case of thought abuse.

19. ***What will a wise child do?***
Make their parents proud of them.

20. ***Fill in the blank: Your folks are God's ___ for you so listen to their point of view.***
Guide.

21. ***What happened in the 'Parent Watch' programme?***
The extraordinary relationship between parent and offspring in the species homo sapiens was investigated.

22. ***What will you have to live with?***
The consequences of what you say.

23. ***Name one of the four tips for the safe use of words in the 'Speech-way code'.***
1. Put your brain in gear before opening your mouth. 2. Look round carefully before pulling away into speech. 3. Never accelerate too quickly. 4. Perform an emergency stop if you begin to lose control of your words.

24. ***Name one of the eight quotations that changed the course of history.***
See 'Quotes & Consequences' cards on page 103.

25. ***Who sent us a message from the great skirting board in the sky?***
A mouse who had been caught by a mouse trap.

26. ***What is MC Solomon's advice about traps?***
Stay well away.

27. ***Name three 'traps' that we should watch out for.***
Pride, selfishness, drugs, etc. (See page 112).

28. ***Name two things that people put their trust in.***
Dogs, job, friends, intelligence, horoscopes.

29. ***How do we know God is trustworthy?***
Because over thousands of years he has passed 'the test of experience'.

30. ***What were MC Solomon's 'final words to say'?***
Trust in God come what may.

Useful information

Useful books

K.T. Aitken, *The Daily Study Bible: Proverbs*
The Saint Andrew Press
A very useful commentary on the book of Proverbs

J.I. Packer, *Knowing God*
Hodder and Stoughton
A thought provoking book to help you have reverence for the Lord, (and hence wisdom).

References

1. **All God's Children,** A report from the General Synod Board of Education & Board of Mission, 1991.

Rise Up, Wise Up Cassette

The *Rise Up, Wise Up* cassette contains all the sound effects and theme music you will need to run the *Rise Up, Wise Up* course. Available from your local Christian bookshop or, in case of difficulty, direct from BRF.
Price £5.99.

order form

PLEASE SEND ME THE FOLLOWING:

			QTY	COST
3088 3	Struck by Jesus (Leaders' Guide)	£5.99		
3085 9	Struck by Jesus (Daily Notes)	£2.50		
	Struck by Jesus (Daily Notes-10 pack)	£20.00		
3276 2	Struck by Jesus (resource pack) (incl.VAT)	£5.99		
3084 0	Out Of This World (Leaders' Guide)	£7.99		
3083 2	Out Of This World (Daily Notes)	£2.99		
	Out Of This World (Daily Notes-10 pack)	£25.00		
3288 6	Out Of This World (audio cassette) (incl.VAT)	£5.99		
3254 1	Getting To Grips With God (Leaders' Guide)	£8.99		
3255 X	Getting To Grips With God (Daily Notes)	£2.99		
	Getting To Grips With God (Daily Notes-10-pack)	£25.00		
3527 3	Getting To Grips With God (audio cassette) (incl.VAT.)	£5.99		
3259 2	Rise Up, Wise Up (Leaders' Guide)	£8.99		
3260 6	Rise Up, Wise Up (Daily Notes)	£2.99		
	Rise Up, Wise Up (Daily Notes-10-pack)	£25.00		
3081 6	**Rise Up, Wise Up (audio cassette)** (incl.VAT.)	£5.99		

Please complete the payment details below (all orders must be accompanied by the appropriate payment) and send your completed form to **BRF, Peter's Way, Sandy Lane West, Oxford OX4 5HG**.

Name ....

Address ....

.... Postcode ....

POSTAGE AND PACKING RATES

ORDER VALUE	UK	EUROPE	REST OF Surface	WORLD Airmail
£6.00 & under	£1.25	£2.25	£2.25	£3.50
£6.01-£14.99	£3.00	£3.50	£4.50	£6.00
£15.00-£29.99	£4.00	£5.50	£7.50	£11.00
£30.00 & over	free	enquire	enquire	enquire

Total value of books: £ ________

Postage and packing: £ ________

Donation to BRF: £ ________

Total enclosed: £ ________

Method of Payment: ☐ Cheque ☐ Mastercard ☐ Visa ☐ Postal Order

Credit card number ☐☐☐☐ ☐☐☐☐ ☐☐☐☐ ☐☐☐☐

Expiry Date ☐☐☐☐

Signature ______________________ Date ____________

The Bible Reading Fellowship, Peter's Way, Sandy Lane West, Oxford OX4 5HG
Tel: 01865 748227 Fax: 01865 773150 BRF is a registered charity (No. 233280)
Prices and postage rates valid until 31 December 1996

PLEASE KEEP ME INFORMED ABOUT BRF YOUNG PEOPLE'S RESOURCES ☐

The Lightning Bolts Series

Now that you have gone through *Rise Up, Wise Up*, you might like to know about other titles in the Lightning Bolts series. Following the same format as *Rise Up, Wise Up*, each course comprises a leaders' guide, resource cassette and daily notes, available from your local Christian bookshop or, in case of difficulty, direct from BRF.

Struck by Jesus

Takes ten incidents from Mark's Gospel and through them examines the extraordinary marks of God's life on earth; from his compassion to his authority, from his gentleness to his obedience.

Out of This World

Out of This World explores ten key themes in God's developing master-plan for the disaster-prone human race. Spanning from Genesis to Revelation it follows the epic history of God's relationship with human beings. The plan of the Master in the face of disaster is a heart-warming tale that is truly 'out of this world'.

Getting to Grips with God

Getting to Grips with God grapples with such questions as: 'Does God exist?'; 'Why am I alive?'; 'What's the big deal about Jesus?'; 'What's the point of being a Christian?'; 'What would it involve anyway?' This course is designed to help your young people's group 'get to grips with God', and is a great introduction to the basics of the Christian faith.

Close Encounters

By introducing you to ten diverse characters who close encounter Jesus in Luke's Gospel, *Close Encounters* will help you and your youth group to close encounter him yourselves.

Upside-Down but the Right Way Round

Upside-Down but the Right Way Round explores the topsy-turvy teaching of Jesus in 'The Sermon on the Mount' with the aim of helping your group grasp its right-way-roundness.

***Struck by Jesus**, **Out of This World** and **Getting to Grips with God** are already published. **Close Encounters** will be available in spring 1997 and **Upside-Down but the Right Way Round** in the autumn of 1997. Please phone the BRF office to confirm prices.*

Rise Up, Wise Up

LEARN THE WISE WAY WITH A PROVERB A DAY

70 Days High Voltage Bible Readings for 11-14 year olds by Nick Jones

Rise Up & *Wise Up* explores seventy wise sayings from the book of Proverbs—an ancient 'wise living' instruction manual for young people. Packed with down to earth advice it will help you discover...

- What you can learn from ants.
- How to be a friend worth having.
- When to put a sock in it.
- What's the most important thing you can do in life.
- How to deal with temper tantrums.
- Why temptation is like a mousetrap.
- How to smack it to your enemies.
- What nasty habits you can catch from your mates.
- How to bring a smile to God's face.

Rise Up & *Wise Up* will help you take on board the wise words of yester-millennium and learn how to be wise today.

This book is one of a number of high-voltage titles in the 'Lightning Bolts' range. Each takes a theme or book from the Bible and explores it in ten weeks of bite-sized Bible readings using a thought-provoking, amusing and hands-on approach to strike home the message.

Available from your youth group leaders or church bookstall.

£2.99

Rise Up, Wise Up

LEARN THE WISE WAY WITH A PROVERB A DAY

70 Days High Voltage Bible Readings for 11-14 year olds by Nick Jones

Rise Up & *Wise Up* explores seventy wise sayings from the book of Proverbs—an ancient 'wise living' instruction manual for young people. Packed with down to earth advice it will help you discover...

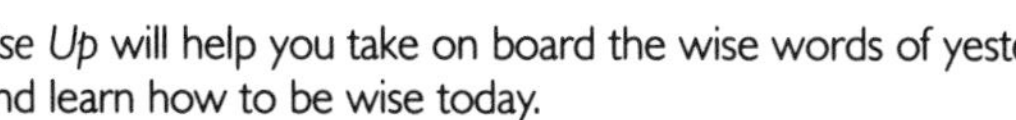

- What you can learn from ants.
- How to be a friend worth having.
- When to put a sock in it.
- What's the most important thing you can do in life.
- How to deal with temper tantrums.
- Why temptation is like a mousetrap.
- How to smack it to your enemies.
- What nasty habits you can catch from your mates.
- How to bring a smile to God's face.

Rise Up & *Wise Up* will help you take on board the wise words of yester-millennium and learn how to be wise today.

This book is one of a number of high-voltage titles in the 'Lightning Bolts' range. Each takes a theme or book from the Bible and explores it in ten weeks of bite-sized Bible readings using a thought-provoking, amusing and hands-on approach to strike home the message.

Available from your youth group leaders or church bookstall.

£2.99

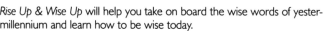